Shakespeare **Thinking**

Shakespeare

Series edited by Simon Palfrey and Ewan Fernie

Shakespeare **Thinking**

Philip Davis

continuum

Continuum
The Tower Building
11 York Road
London
SE1 7NX
www.continuumbooks.com

80 Maiden Lane
Suite 704
New York
NY 10038

British Library Cataloguing-in-Publication Data
A catalogue record for this book is available from the British Library.

ISBN-10: HB: 0-8264-8694-0
        PB: 0-8264-8695-9
ISBN-13: HB: 9780826486943
        PB: 9780826486950

Library of Congress Cataloging-in-Publication Data
A catalog record for this book is available from the Library of Congress.

Typeset by BookEns Ltd, Royston, Herts

For Jenny Sanders
and in memory of Wil
'The loss is as yourself, great'

Contents

Acknowledgements

The text used here, unless otherwise stated, is *The Oxford Shakespeare: The Complete Works*, edited by J. Jowett, W. Montgomery, G. Taylor and S. Wells, second edition (Oxford: Oxford University Press, 2005).

I wish to thank Brian Nellist and those congenial editors, Ewan Fernie and Simon Palfrey, for thoughts and talks, together with Jonathan Bate for putting me on to brain scanners. Neil Roberts at Liverpool and Guillaume Thierry at Bangor have patiently taken me further into the brain and I am glad of my partnership with them and with my language colleague Victorina Gonzalez-Diaz. Also never forgetting Wilbur Sanders to whom, always with Jenny, this book is dedicated.

Philip Davis
School of English, University of Liverpool
August 2006

General Editors' Preface

Shakespeare Now! represents a new form for new approaches. Whereas academic writing is far too often ascendant and detached, attesting all too clearly to years of specialist training, *Shakespeare Now!* offers a series of intellectual adventure stories: animate with fresh and often exposed thinking, with ideas still heating in the mind.

This series of 'minigraphs' will thus help to bridge two yawning gaps in current public discourse. First, the gap between scholarly thinking and a public audience: the assumption of academics that they cannot speak to anyone but their peers unless they hopelessly dumb-down their work. Second, the gap between public audience and scholarly thinking: the assumption of regular playgoers, readers, or indeed actors that academics write about the plays at a level of abstraction or specialization that they cannot hope to understand.

But accessibility should not be mistaken for comfort or predictability. Impatience with scholarly obfuscation is usually accompanied by a basic impatience with anything but (supposed) common sense. What this effectively means is a distrust of really thinking, and a disdain for anything that might unsettle conventional assumptions, particularly through crossing or re-drafting formal, political, or theoretical boundaries. We encourage such adventure, and base our claim to a broad audience upon it.

Here, then, is where our series is innovative: no compromising of the sorts of things that can be thought; a commitment to publishing powerful cutting-edge scholarship; *but* a conviction that these things are essentially communicable, that we can find a language that is enterprising, individual and shareable.

To achieve this we need a form that can capture the genuine challenge and vigour of thinking. Shakespeare is intellectually exciting, and so too are the ideas and debates that thinking about his work can provoke. But published scholarship often fails to communicate much of this. It is difficult to sustain excitement over the 80–120,000 words customary for a monograph: difficult enough for the writer, and perhaps even more so for the reader. Scholarly articles have likewise become a highly formalized mode not only of publication, but also of intellectual production. The brief length of articles means that a concept can be outlined, but its implications or application can rarely be tested in detail. The decline of sustained, exploratory attention to the singularity of a play's language, occasion, or movement is one of the unfortunate results. Often 'the play' is somehow assumed, a known and given thing that is not really worth exploring. So we spend our time pursuing collateral contexts: criticism becomes a belated, historicizing footnote.

Important things have got lost. Above all, any vivid sense as to why we are bothered with these things in the first place. Why read? Why go to plays? Why are they important? How does any pleasure they give relate to any of the things we labour to say about them? In many ways, literary criticism has forgotten affective and political immediacy. It has assumed a shared experience of the plays and then averted the gaze from any such experience, or any testing of it. We want a more ductile and sensitive mode of production; one that has more chance of capturing what people are really thinking and reading about, rather than what the pre-empting imperatives of journal or respectable monograph tend to encourage.

Furthermore, there is a vast world of intellectual possiblity – from the past and present – that mainstream Shakespeare criticism has all but ignored. In recent years there has been a move away from 'theory' in literary studies: an aversion to its obscure jargon and complacent self-regard; a sense that its tricks were too easily rehearsed and that the whole game has become one of diminishing returns. This has further encouraged a retreat into the supposed safety of historicism. Of course the best such work is stimulating, revelatory, and indispensable. But too often there is little trace of any struggle; little sense that the writer is coming at the subject afresh, searching for the most appropriate language or method. Alternatively, the prose is so labored that all trace of an urgent story is quite lost.

We want to open up the sorts of thinking – and thinkers – that might help us get at what Shakespeare is doing or why Shakespeare matters. This might include psychology, cognitive science, theology, linguistics, phenomenology, metaphysics, ecology, history, political theory; it can mean other art forms such as music, sculpture, painting, dance; it can mean the critical writing itself becomes a creative act.

In sum, we want the minigraphs to recover what the Renaissance 'essay' form was originally meant to embody. It meant an 'assay' – a trial or a test of something; putting something to the proof; and doing so in a form that is not closed-off and that cannot be reduced to a system. We want to communicate intellectual activity at its most alive: when it is still exciting to the one doing it; when it is questing and open, just as Shakespeare is. Literary criticism – that is, really thinking about words in action, plays as action – can start making a much more creative and vigorous contribution to contemporary intellectual *life*.

Simon Palfrey and Ewan Fernie

1 The Original Text

I claim that there is such a thing as Shakespearean thinking which somehow feels like no other. In 1817, in *Characters of Shakespear's Plays*, the critic William Hazlitt had written of *Hamlet*: 'Other dramatic writers give us very fine versions or paraphrases of nature: but Shakespear, together with his own comments, gives us the original text, that we may judge for ourselves.' This present book[1] is about the way that Shakespeare's drama is indeed an original text or background script for the creation of life – an argument made not in the spirit of bardolatry, but on behalf of recognizing in the plays a genuine mental template for evolutionary creation, a linguistic equivalent of the structuring work of DNA. For, like DNA, the original text hidden within the workings of Shakespeare is a text not so much to be read or explained as to be activated in a life-form.

Paraphrase is no good here, in its pat normalizing of the meaning of experience. For Shakespeare's drama generates a language creatively anterior to, and more primary than, mere paraphrase – where paraphrase means the approximate re-description of what is supposed to be already there, the subsequent laying on of pre-established opinion, the language of the mere second-order aftermath. And paraphrase is what we mainly do, not just in literary criticism but in existence: secondary creatures not getting back to the heart and root of the matter as if for the first time again, but just putting received things into other words, knowingly repeating the already known in another version. It is what Berowne in *Love's Labour's Lost* might cheekily call one of the 'slow arts' of education that 'entirely keep the brain'. What he wants instead is a quicker, more physically dispersed form of mentality that is not 'immuréd in the brain':

> But with the motion of all elements
> Courses as swift as thought in every power,
> And gives to every power a double power,
> Above their functions and their offices.
> It adds a precious seeing to the eye ...

4.3.305–9

Thus, this book is also about the way that Shakespeare, eschewing paraphrase, does something almost directly physical within the human brain, doubling the mental effect of his plays.

But if in the name of a stranger primary reality, that thinking process is in no sense straightforward – is, rather non-linear in its account of experience; untethered to the regular consequential spaces between propositions; traversing instead multiple space-times simultaneously – then the following out of that thinking cannot be straightforward either. If we cannot wholly explain our way back into Shakespeare's time or Shakespeare's mind, because too much is lost, distorted or went unspoken, there is in that a licence for help wherever we can get it, in the alternative and less orthodox histories of human thinking. The history of Shakespearean thinking after Shakespeare – the attempt to hold onto all that Shakespeare can stand for within the structure of the human mind, as the paradigm of the dramatically thinking poet – that informal history, I say, is a partial, broken, fragmented and scattered thing, in the light of the pressures for the normalization of thought. We need to accept the sporadic clues and incipient re-openings anywhere we can find them – from different times, from different forms of writing – in order to reassemble and decode more of his underlying script. For what is at stake here is the struggle to re-establish broad, rough lines of communication back through time, in the face of a danger so substantial as to give some licence for risk: namely, the danger of a potentially otherwise lost but vital form of human mentality called, in this shorthand, 'Shakespearean'.[2]

*

We may think we know what Shakespeare means – for however historically distant, his is still, we suppose, our language. But deep in Shakespeare's language there are hints and secrets of creation, things half-lost to us or half-forgotten, which lie anterior to our familiarization of his meaning. And these hidden things have been kept for centuries. Indeed, there is evidence that even by the middle of the seventeenth century the mental leaps that characterize Shakespearean thinking were ever increasingly a thing of the past, at least according to the then current literary theory. Abraham Cowley, examining the Bible in the light of translations from the previous century, the age of Shakespeare, said that 'the old fashion of writing was like *Disputing in Enthymemes*, where half is left out to be supplied by the Hearer; ours is like *Syllogisms*, where all that is meant is exprest'. It is an Enlightenment model of thinking which, arguably, has dominated our ideas of thinking for ever after. In his 'Notes to a Pindaric paraphrase of Isaiah chapter 34', Cowley describes in contrast to contemporary rationalism the want of transitions, the sudden breaks and leaps, in Isaiah's text:

> The manner of the *Prophets* writing, especially of *Isaiah*, seems to me very like that of *Pindar*; they pass from one thing to another with almost *Invisible connexions*, and are full of words and expressions of the highest and boldest flights of *Poetry*, as may be seen in this Chapter, where there are as extraordinary Figures as can be found in any *Poet* whatsoever; and the connexion is so difficult, that I am forced to adde a little, and leave out a great deal to make it seem Sense to us, who are not used to that elevated way of expression.

Cowley's proposed revision is close to what lies behind Dryden's rewritings of a seemingly rough, verbally obscure, slap-dash Shakespeare, in order to create one clear, sensible perspective – because, says Dryden, 'there must be a point of sight in which all the lines terminate', making all the thoughts come fittingly together, rather than a simultaneous variety of contrary passions 'ever crossing and jostling each other out of the way' ('The Grounds of Criticism in Tragedy'). To Dryden, Shakespeare's work was not of a 'finished' character.[3]

But the grammar of rapid transitions and invisible connections still remained within the English Bible. There is no doubt that Shakespeare emerges out of a particular rich moment in the history and evolution of the language, a moment not only shared with but also partly created by the translators of the Bible and, what is more, itself informed by the ancient ways of thought and expression recreated in that translation. It was the Authorized Version in particular, coming as it did out of the same language-pool as did Shakespeare himself, that preserved the memory of an otherwise almost abandoned language – in secular contexts a language increasingly known, if known at all, only under the specialist heading of 'the sublime'. A key figure in this story of a language half-lost, half-unacknowledged is Bishop Robert Lowth in his effort to recover an understanding of the procedures of the Bible's Hebrew poetry.

In his *Lectures on the Sacred Poetry of the Hebrews* (1753) Lowth noted that the common prose language of the Hebrews was 'connected by the continued succession of the different parts', the order of the words 'regular and uniform', so that 'nothing appears inconsistent, abrupt, or confused' (lecture 14). But Hebrew poetry was different: the dramatic sorrow of Job, for instance, 'bursts forth on a sudden, and flows from his heart, where it had long been confined and suppressed' (3.3–4) – the translation is Lowth's own from the Hebrew:

> Let the day perish, I was born in it
> And the night [which] said, A man is conceived.
> That night – let darkness seize upon it

'Doubtless,' says Lowth of that last line, the author 'intended to express himself first in this manner – "Be that night darkness".' 'But,' says Lowth, 'in the very act of uttering it, he suddenly catches at an expression which appears more animated and energetic.' An officious grammarian, he adds, might take in hand such a passage – 'and all the impetuosity and ardour would in a moment be extinguished'. After all, the reader will acknowledge that Job's essential meaning is clear – 'so clear indeed, that if any person should attempt to make it more copious and explanatory, he would render it less expressive of the mind and feelings of the speaker'. Indeed, there is, Lowth notes, a passage in Jeremiah (20.14–15) 'so exactly similar, that it might almost be imagined a direct imitation'. The meaning is much the same – or there is little difference in phraseology:

> Cursed be the day on which I was born;
> The day on which my mother bare me, let it not be
> blessed.
> Cursed be the man who brought the news to my
> father,
> Saying, There is a man child born unto thee;
> Making him exceedingly glad.

But Jeremiah 'fills up the ellipses, smooths and harmonises the rough and uncouth language of Job' and thus 'the imprecation of Jeremiah has more in it of complaint than of indignation; it is milder, softer, and more plaintive, peculiarly calculated to excite pity, in moving which the great excellence of this prophet exists; while that of Job is more adapted to strike us with terror'. The poetry of the Hebrews, and of Job in particular, concludes Lowth, abounds with phrases and idioms which 'frequently appear to us harsh and unusual, I had almost said unnatural and barbarous; which, however, are destitute neither of meaning nor of force, were we but sufficiently informed to judge of their true application' (lecture 14). The poet never remained 'fixed to a single point', but 'glances continually from one object to another', in sudden emotions or new states of mind, and frequent variation of tenses. Lowth's scholarship here recovers the meaning of pre-verbal space in the midst of writing – space in which there lodges the inner mental voice that tacitly leads the thinking from one level to another. And what he retrieves from Job, we can find to multiply again and again in Shakespeare.

Shakespeare did not need formally to know or state any such principle of connectivity: he only needed to find it and use it; practically, intuitively, variously. It is everywhere embodied in his processes, but processes which are also latent in what Melville called Shakespeare's 'back-ground': a darkness out of which came 'those deep far-away things in him; those occasional flashings-forth of the intuitive Truth in him; those short, quick probings at the very axis of reality' which appear 'covertly and in snatches':

> And few of his endless commentators and critics seem to have remembered, or even perceived, that the immediate products of a great mind are not so great, as that undeveloped, (and sometimes undevelopable), yet dimly discernible greatness, to which these immediate products are but the infallible indices. In Shakespeare's tomb lies infinitely more than Shakespeare ever wrote.[4]

This is like the portrait of Achilles half-hidden behind his spear in *The Rape of Lucrece*: 'For much imaginary work was there | ... himself behind | Was left unseen save to the eye of mind; | A hand, a foot, a face, a leg, a head, | Stood for the whole to be imagined' (1422, 1425–8). No formal history can recover or develop the full background to such a world-view, deducible only in nascent glimpses. For Shakespeare's way of thinking was never fully formalized in the first place, because it couldn't be – it was dynamic, not programmatic, it was a template of eclectic possibilities. And so in Shakespeare the template was not so much articulated as activated by means of dramatic testings, a performative process of thought itself consonant with the *implicit* world-view from which it derives.

To Carlyle in *On Heroes and Hero Worship* (1840), as to many Romantics and post-Romantics, Shakespeare was like a rich latent resource awaiting further realization: there is 'more in Shakspeare's intellect than we have yet seen. It is what I call an unconscious intellect; there is more virtue in it than he himself is aware of'. Much 'lies hid' in Shakespeare, said Carlyle, 'much that was not known at all, not speakable at all'. That means that 'the latest generations of men will find new meanings in Shakspeare; new elucidations of their own human being; new harmonies with the infinite structure of the Universe; concurrences with later ideas'. And why so? Not for the sake of reading into Shakespeare the latest fancy idea; but because his creations still seem to embody unnamed laws, secrets and patterns as from deep in the origin of things. On reading *Hamlet*, Emerson, friend of Carlyle, said that it had taken until the nineteenth century for human beings truly to begin to apprehend Shakespeare. In *Representative Men* (1850), he concluded that Shakespeare was 'a full man' – a man who transcended the vehicle and genre in which he worked – and 'wrote the text of modern life'.

This capacity to burst into ever-new activations of itself is a crucial evolutionary component in Shakespeare's 'original text', not to be left behind in the subsequent refinements of rational clarity. You can sense these strange hidden laws of his, experientially, but only when they are in operation. So, for example, when Laertes laments the madness of his sister after the death of their father, you can feel that something deeply secret in the whole thinking of the play has momentarily surfaced:

> O heavens, is't possible a young maid's wits
> Should be as mortal as an old man's life?
> Nature is fine in love, and where 'tis fine
> It sends some precious instance of itself
> After the thing it loves.
>
> *Hamlet*, 4.5.160–5

Dr Johnson dismissed these lines as obscure and affected, and at least one modern editor thinks the contrived idea to be rather absurd. But something seems to be coming through here. When I know that 'fine' means 'sensitive', I can paraphrase the meaning: a part of you seems to enter the person you love; something in Ophelia's mind dies in and with her father. So, we are all affected by loss of, or damage to, someone we care about. And then the tamed thing calms down into a normalized secondary meaning.

But the meaning was not like that in the first dramatic moment of its happening. It wasn't a static, separate statement. Yet it was indeed an *it*, an earlier almost pre-human force within the human set-up: an 'it' in us that sends 'some instance of *itself*' after the thing it loves. And, what is more, this 'it' recalls another such instance of itself in the play, lines earlier, when Claudius, feeling something of this in his own fears too, spoke thus of 'sorrows in battalions':

> poor Ophelia
> Divided from herself and her fair judgment,
> Without the which we are pictures or mere beasts

> 4.5.82–4

'*Divided* from *herself*': suddenly you see Shakespeare really means it and, at once, more than it. That is to say, whatever goes into this belongs to something *more* underlying it that comes out again in different places. For at such points his words feel like things, like symbols of tacitly connected thought in need of decoding, and not like transparencies. As Ophelia is divided from her very self, there are now two people here in lines 82–4 – 'poor Ophelia' (whoever that now is, be it in her or in others' memories of her), 'herself', and that sanity of judgment which makes the difference between the two. It is this mind of hers that is gone into the thought of some-one else instead by line 165. Putting these different lines together – or rather letting these things resonate across space and time, mov-ing their thought in and out of separate persons and different bodies – is what it means to find the underlying code or language of the play. Here, 'language' is no longer of course merely the words used, like 'pictures', but means the working out of the impulsive laws of the whole underlying matrix, the very shapes and spaces and niches out of which all things come into being in the drama. It is a maximal language – 'a young maid's wits' thus expanding the particular to the very brink of the general – which makes Ophelia an instance of *it*, amid the ever-growing squadrons of human sorrows, rather than it being in descriptive service to Ophelia alone.

In Shakespeare it is not character that speaks, originally or finally, but a life-force, as anterior to character as it is prior to explicit theme or conceptualized agenda, which is entrusted to work itself out.

Hazlitt's dynamic

It is with Hazlitt that my story of half-lost scripts really begins. For Hazlitt himself had hoped for better than a life of mere literary paraphrase. 'Early in life,' he wrote in his *Letter to William Gifford*, 'I had made (what I thought) a metaphysical discovery.' The discovery was the basis of his publication of *An Essay on the Principles of Human Action*, in 1805 at the age of 27.[5] The new thought which the essay passionately struggled to articulate was that human beings were not, in the *first* place, separate, self-contained and static creatures, programmed to be brutally and instinctively selfish, and increasingly liable to calculate everything steadily in advance in terms of their own self-interest. That was the world suggested by philosophers such as Thomas Hobbes, a world which seemed to Hazlitt one of those belated paraphrases heavily imposed upon our nature as an idea of ourselves. What we were – before all the names and the concepts – was something originally quicker and more innocent than that. Our primal feelings snatched at whatever was good and of benefit – before ever we knew whether it was our good or the good of others, or even the distinction between the two. Identity, the solidification of selfhood comes later, with memory. But for Hazlitt the underlying primary impulse is never to do with the past but with the future. And the future is by definition not yet here, a thing unknown and to be created, if indeed it is to be a genuine future and not the present or the past in continuance. That is why there can be almost *no time* in the movement of our primary impulses – they are instant, barely present, anticipatory between the moment and the future imagined for itself. The sudden opening of possibility gives a split-second chance of creating a new future by acting quickly towards the realizing of it. That is what feelings are in Hazlitt, instinctively thinking energies always seeking to convert themselves immediately into the very actions they have a bare second to conceive.

But the *Essay*, reported Hazlitt years later, 'fell still-born from the press'. It is one of the more-or-less *lost* works of human thinking: a work which sought a philosophical language by which to hold open the momentary, passing secrets of mental working for more permanent scrutiny – and, perhaps unsurprisingly in view of the paradox involved, failed in the attempt. What this early failure of his greatest discovery meant for Hazlitt was an irony for ever after – a life subsequently spent writing occasional essays which were not of the obscure, dynamic and metaphysical nature of the original *Essay*, but more personal and self-reflective, more accessibly conversational, and thus, above all, more essentially second-order, according to the very principles of the *Essay* itself.

Yet the great botched *An Essay on the Principles of Human Action*, though abandoned even by Hazlitt himself, survived implicitly in one place: in Hazlitt's interest in writing about Shakespeare's plays. The sheer *gusto* of those writings (to use one of Hazlitt's own favourite terms) arises out of the wrecked system half-deducible behind them, the insights like scattered hints and fragments from the past suddenly finding a renewed future for themselves. It is those hints that I wish to develop, as a basis for learning the deep language of Shakespearean thinking.

To Hazlitt, Shakespeare's plays are not set scripts or finished productions, any more than our own identities are, but creations coming into being through rehearsals of themselves, experiments in human nature, at a deep level prior to conscious plan or concept.[6] What Shakespeare became to Hazlitt was the essentially dramatic

life-force celebrated in the *Essay* as prior to settled separate identities. To describe that creative force, and to have it recognized as
something more than just literary, what Hazlitt needed was not the
language of the theatre or the language of metaphysics he had
attempted before, but the language of science:

> In Shakspeare there is a continual composition and decomposi-
> tion of its elements, a fermentation of every particle in the whole
> mass, by its alternate affinity or antipathy to other principles,
> which are brought in contact with it. Till the experiment is tried,
> we do not know the result, the turn which the character will take
> in its new circumstances.
>
> *Lectures on the English Poets*, 'On Shakspeare and Milton'

To Hazlitt, Shakespeare was what used to be called a 'natural
philosopher', from a time before the separation of arts and
sciences, of physics, magic, philosophy and poetry. What Hazlitt's
Shakespeare offers is a world held in dense liquid solution within
his laboratory, an atomic forcefield or an elemental melting-pot of
language, in which nothing and no one is securely separate from
anything else. In *Characters of Shakespear's Plays*, Hazlitt made an
important distinction between Chaucer's mind and Shakespeare's in
terms of their respective shaping principles. Chaucer's mind in the
Canterbury Tales was consecutive and continuous, doing one thing
at a time, passing from one to another along the road of pilgrimage.
But Shakespeare's was essentially non-linear: he saw everything acting and re-acting together, and coexisting at once, the mutual inter-
actions of dialogue and of metaphor being characteristic of the
mind. Although kept under pressure of forward development from
first scene through to last, the Shakespearean performative shape
was closer to circle than to line.

What is more, within that space, in the 'continual composition
and decomposition' of the whole, it is not only that one element
may bounce off another outside it, but also that one element, or one
person even, may suddenly find another within it. Leontes, for

example, commands Antigonus to take the newly born daughter of his wife, 'this female bastard' lying at his feet, to a remote place outside his lands

> and that there thou leave it,
> Without more mercy, to it own protection
> And favour of the climate.
>
> *The Winter's Tale*, 2.3.177–8

Yet what we hear coming through Leontes, even as he seeks to staunch them, are those unvoiced and unheard cries for 'mercy' and 'protection' and 'favour'. Sometimes thought in Shakespeare is so powerful in its language that the object of the thought, at a level prior to personality, becomes more present than the person thinking it. By a species of osmosis, the invisible thought passes through the apparently impermeable membrane of skin, making the boundaries between characters less sure, like the storm at once outside and inside Lear's head. In his 1812 lecture 'On Liberty and Necessity', one of his later diluted rewrites of the great *Essay*, Hazlitt makes clear that no one exists unconditionally in independent freedom, no agent acts without suffering. To Hazlitt, in the dense medium of life human beings are thus either what he calls *transmitters*, merely passing on the pressures around them, or *reactors* who, as the external pressures bear upon them, draw upon such inner resources as they have to resist and modify the forces moving through them. Till the Shakespearean experiment is complete, no one knows which is which or what form the pressures will assume.

In the great immanent experiment Hazlitt thus describes, it is not so much that Shakespeare started with 'ideas'; rather, he started by feeling out those originating places, by creating those spatial situations which thoughts themselves come out of. What Hazlitt understood was the importance of the spatial set-up from which Shakespeare began:

> Within the circle of dramatic character and natural passion, each individual is to feel as keenly, as profoundly, as rapidly as

possible, but he is not to feel beyond it, for others or for the whole. Each character, on the contrary, must be a kind of centre of repulsion to the rest; and it is their hostile interests brought into collision, that must tug at their heart-strings, and call forth every faculty of thought, of speech, and action. They must not be represented like a set of profiles, looking all the same way, nor with their faces turned round to the audience; but in dire contention with each other: their words, like their swords, must strike fire from one another.[7]

Fullness is the first principle of life in Shakespeare, fullness in what Hazlitt calls mobile 'fermentation', every space occupied with the struggle between centres of vitality and with the burgeoning language it calls forth. Even in conflict, the characters work in mutuality upon each other. The first sign of life for Shakespeare is that there is always *more* than he or anyone can control, and that is what he first wants and ever works for.[8] This is drama in language 'struck out at a heat, on the spur of the occasion' ('On Shakspeare and Milton'): there is no roomy place or time of ease for secondary social adjustments or calculations. There is, as Hazlitt might say, a law of physics involved: 'One fire drives out one fire, one nail, one nail' (*Coriolanus*, 4.7.54).

> Even as one heat another heat expels,
> Or as one nail by strength drives out another,
> So the remembrance of my former love
> Is by a newer object quite forgotten.
>
> *The Two Gentlemen of Verona*, 2.4.190–3

These are experiments which call forth a world that comes into being as if for the first time. Like words within rhyme-schemes in early Shakespeare, things have to adapt to the places available to them. As the characters face each other, the very space between them itself becomes a third presence, like the Grecian urn emergent between profiles in a *trompe d'oeil* drawing of double perspective. Shakespeare loves even-handedly working in those charged and saturated places in between two figures. They mark the point at which the stage is not just full of people but also of forces, of life, moving in and out of them. Such dynamic 'spaces between' call for human expression from the people around them, having at once half-generated those characters and been half-created by them. It is like the taut space between Coriolanus and his family near the end of the play, into which his mother pushes his son; or the terrible gap between Leontes and Hermione in which Mamilius played so uncomfortably, 'drooped, took it deeply | Fastened and fixed the shame on't in himself' (*The Winter's Tale*, 2.3.14–15). And one of the names that in-between space, which I have also called the third thing, finds for itself is 'confusion': 'When two authorities are up, | Neither supreme, how soon confusion | May enter 'twixt the gap of both and take | The one by th'other' (*Coriolanus*, 3.1.112–15).

Something of the richness involved in such 'confusion', tragic or comic, may be suggested when one realizes, for example, the electrical connection between *this* moment from early in *As You Like It* when Celia urges the slight young Orlando not to take on the champion wrestler Charles:

> Young gentleman, your spirits are too bold for your years: you have seen cruel proof of this man's strength. If you saw yourself with your eyes or knew yourself with your judgement, the fear of your adventure would counsel you to a more equal enterprise.

> 1.2.162–6

And *this* thought, near the end of the play, from Orlando himself on seeing his brother win a bride so easily in Celia when he cannot, it seems, with Rosalind:

> They shall be married tomorrow and I will bid the Duke to the nuptial. But O, how bitter a thing it is to look into happiness through another man's eyes.

> 5.2.41–2.

In complex ways that can be worked out only afterwards, 'If you saw yourself with *your* eyes' and 'to look into happiness through *another* man's eyes' [my italics] are like Hazlitt's vibrating 'particles' communicating to each other across the full, involved mind-space of the play. This too is a language of the play, a wider grammar, with Orlando caught thus between 'his own' and 'another's'. Each individual is to feel to the maximum of himself, said Hazlitt, but still cannot reach the whole. First, Celia is Orlando's eyes, then Orlando is his brother's, without either ceasing to be simultaneously themselves too: for so often in Shakespeare people find themselves in two places at once. 'If you saw yourself with your eyes' thus requires another self, one that is other to 'yourself' as well as the same; equally, 'To look into happiness with another man's eyes' requires that you also be somebody else, yet at your own felt expense. What is opened here within the self and between selves is exactly a space of thought, with the formal relationship between the self-estrangement of self-reflection and the leap of both empathy and envy left undecided but available for thinking.

Thus, when they pick up on it, the sudden coming together of these two moments, from Act 1 and Act 5, leaves readers and spectators seeing *more* than they know they could if they were one of the characters before them – which for a moment they are as well. It leaves them dizzyingly seeing more, I say, than they feel they have quite a right to or a capacity for, when thinking simply as separate individuals. That is when they are in the thick of the sheer life on the stage and mentally extended in the way Shakespeare most wants. For what I have called the third thing, arising out of the spaces between the characters, is also, as in Hamlet, a sort of 'it' which, non-human or pre-human, also gradually creates the form of the whole.

In a sense, that 'it' is the main and most important being in the play, though it is there only in process. Agamemnon describes it in his own complacent way – but then that is what Shakespeare loves to do: to disguise one of his absolute secrets within the relative position of a partial character, but also to add a more powerful language to take it just a step beyond partiality:

> checks and disasters
> Grow in the veins of actions highest rear'd,
> As knots, by the conflux of meeting sap,
> Infects the sound pine and diverts his grain
> Tortive and errant from his course of growth …
> Sith every action that hath gone before
> Whereof we have record, trial did draw
> Bias and athwart, not answering the aim
> And that unbodied figure of the thought
> That gave't surmised shape.
>
> *Troilus and Cressida*, 1.3.4–16

Here it is only in a speech and almost betrayed by its own embodiment. But in the play itself, that shift and swerve away from merely human aims is the work of some strange unbodied thought immanently seeking a shape for itself in the wider working-out of the drama. It *is* the play, but it thinks not as we do but only through the actual process of forming itself.

What Hazlitt helps us to recognize is that Shakespeare's experiments are deeply morphological. Everything is thrown into the melting pot to take its chance, and whatever comes out again, under the pressure of each contingency, does so anew without explicit intent, lost and found in an improvised replication of life's creative process – the finite full of what is near infinite and almost too much for it. A final sense of what it might feel like to have the mentality of this sort of excited Romantic reader of Shakespeare may be given not by Hazlitt himself but, more introspectively, by Goethe. Here is his young enthusiast, Wilhelm Meister, in Carlyle's translation of 1824, rehearsing Hamlet and himself finding infinite space in a nutshell:

> He lived and moved in the Shakspearean world, feeling or knowing nothing but the movements of his own mind.

We have heard of some Enchanter summoning, by magic for-
mulas, a vast multitude of spiritual shapes into his cell. The con-
jurations are so powerful that the whole space of the apartment
is quickly full; and the spirits crowding on to the verge of the
little circle which they must not pass, around this, and above the
master's head, keep increasing in number, and ever whirling in
perpetual transformation. Every corner is crammed, every crevice
is possessed. Embryos expand themselves, and giant forms con-
tract into the size of nuts ...
So sat Wilhelm in his privacy; with unknown movements, a
thousand feelings and capacities awoke in him, of which he for-
merly had neither notion nor anticipation.

Wilhelm Meister's Apprenticeship, Book 3, Chapter 9

It is as though the movements in this one mind follow the patterns
through which all minds are created – as with the deposed King
Richard II in his prison – each thought a potential life of its own.
Shakespeare seems intuitively to love what these days we would call
a Mandelbrot fractal: a generated self-symmetry working through
varied recursion, like the two sets of twins in *A Comedy of Errors* or
the two sets of lovers in *A Midsummer Night's Dream*; a life-shape
reconfigured within ever smaller sub-divisions of itself; a part thus
containing within itself almost to bursting-point the fundamental
pattern of its larger whole.

I want now to try to go on from Hazlitt's *Essay* – as he himself
hardly could, and therefore without him. And here comes the risk
of discontinuity – of leaving something behind in order to pick it
up again in another form that may take it further forward; of going
sometimes forward, but sometimes also backward in time – in
search of ways of experiencing reality, reactivated by Shakespeare,
that otherwise have become half-lost or half-strange to us.

All Things Flow, Everything Moves

I am not simply saying that, individually, Shakespeare happened to be endlessly inventive. I am saying that his language locked into the very structures of creation. A thought came to Shakespeare, in the way that things happened in the world he figured. And thus he makes creative thinking not just a literary matter but a force in the *world* expressive of all that goes into the making of life.

Of course, Shakespeare could be anything. There is part of him that belongs with Pico della Mirandola's creation myth in *On the Dignity of Man*, where Pico declares that after everything was complete upon earth, God longed for a creature consciously to look upon the creation, as its final expression. That was the origin of man. But all creation was now filled up, everything had been apportioned to the highest, the middle and the lowest orders. 'Finally the Great Artisan ordained that man, to whom He could give nothing belonging only to himself, should share in common whatever properties had been peculiar to each of the other creatures. He received man, therefore, as a creature of undetermined nature.'[9] For Pico, the very map and plan in operation from top to bottom of the creation was replicated from head to toe within the little world of the body of man. This meant that human beings could find within themselves the *feeling* of almost anything, animate or inanimate, in creation: they could find within themselves the equivalence of being anything. It must be said that this imagined power suits Shakespeare well: Coriolanus is 'a thing of blood', 'a thing | Made by some other deity than nature', which thing in him could become beast or god or even planet, without ever being man (*Coriolanus*, 2.2.109; 4.6.94–5). A language of almost physical invocation – so richly 'undetermined' itself as to create a second universe mapped onto the first – is what calls into being those mental possibilities and actualizes them. When Lear cries to those who stand around seeing Cordelia dead, 'O you are men of STONES', it is not metaphor, 'stones' are what he feels these 'men' have become in the

universe (*King Lear*, 5.3.253). You could become anything: he himself cries 'Howl, howl, howl, howl!' like the wounded beast he physically becomes for a moment in crying like that. These are visceral
meanings: to say them is not only to feel them but to become them.
When Lady Macbeth invokes the spirits to invade and 'make thick
my blood, | Stop up th'access and passage to remorse' (*Macbeth*,
1.5.43–4), she is trying to locate herself in a part of her body,
change that body shape, and then think and speak from out of it,
the physical ('blood') right up against the spiritual ('remorse') until
the word 'passage' feels like a thick verbal vein.[10] All this potential
must lie somewhere in Shakespeare's scheme of things.

But still, Shakespeare's implicit cosmology cannot be Pico's.
Shakespeare's power of creation is not just a matter of *free* acts of
will, choice and desire. As Hazlitt recognized, for Shakespeare there
remain problems of space and room and pressure. And these problems are themselves productive: they make an engine to creativity,
creating the need speedily to use the little room available to large
resources before it closes up. Even in their resistance, then, these
constraints are a part of the pressurized cauldron of confinement in
which Shakespeare finds and forces a compressed scope. He is like
the representative man caught between the closed, fixed medieval
universe and the greater capacity for openings and movements
offered by the Renaissance. It is a predicament that helps us see why
Lucretius's *De Rerum Natura* would reappear in the sixteenth century with its claim that there are always tiny interstitial spaces for
the movement of atoms within the world. For, in Shakespeare, there
is constantly both resistance and mutation, change and limit, tiny
spaces and taut pressures, working off each other in productive conflict, as in a system that he has set going, without knowing how long
it can sustain its own tensions. That is why, in the effort to work
ourselves back into Shakespeare's implicit and unformulated mind-
set, nineteenth-century evolutionary theory can be a useful, partial
analogy, where constraint is itself a creative force.

✳

That is also why I want to take Hazlitt's keen sense of Shakespeare as the chemical and biological experimenter forward, towards that great paradigm-shift later in his century, which gives the primary energies of Hazlitt's Shakespearean world the proper perspective of a cosmic drama.

In *The Influence of Darwin on Philosophy* (1910), John Dewey argued that Darwin said of species what, in the prelude to Shakespeare's own age, Copernicus and Galileo had said of the earth – namely, 'It moves'. Species were not separate, were not fixed: they evolved out of each other, in time, across the boundaries, even as the geologist Charles Lyell showed that the earth's surface itself had moved and changed over unimaginable tracts of time. The closed and fixed world of Aristotle, said Dewey, was now more open and more fluid. In lieu of the static taxonomy of millions of different species, instead of all that counting and labelling of minutely different types and faculties, what Darwin offered was a dynamic transformational economy: infinite variation arising out of finite origins. That is why Victorian thinkers such as John Tyndall and W. H. Mallock and Victorian poets such as Arnold and Tennyson looked back to earlier, pre-Christian and long-neglected naturalist cosmologists, such as Heraclitus and the poet-scientist Lucretius, whose theory of colliding atoms, taken from Epicurus, offered an equivalent economy of self-modification. They needed those earlier, near-forgotten models of a radically alternative cosmology.

For the long-dominant model for knowledge was far different from what was now being disclosed by the implications of evolutionary theory. Classically, Dewey noted, knowledge had been equated with its claims for locating what was permanent – laws, fixed forms, final causes which explained the processes of time in terms of the extra-temporal structures which ordered it from above. This is what Bergson in *Creative Evolution* (1907) was to call the *spatializing* of time, taking life out of the living, passing element of its happening and into mind's frozen conceptualizations – turning time itself, for example, into the artificially separated blocks of past, present, future. Classically, what was immutable and immune from the influence of other things had been deemed ontologically higher than what merely changed or was dependent. Life was a top-down structure. In Plato, and even in Aristotle, change was to do with flux and lapse at ground level, with those mingled contingent happenings of mere chance and accident which apparently escaped and insulted intelligence by having no permanent category or single cause in terms of which to explain them.[11] But now, said Dewey and Bergson, intelligence had to take the lessons of biology into itself, into the thinking of the human mind which had evolved out of it. Life was a structure which worked from below upwards, not planned beforehand but evolving onwards. Intelligence had to think again, in terms of processes rather than blocks.

What becomes formulated out of this change came to be known as 'process philosophy'. It was developed in the early twentieth century, not only through John Dewey and Henri Bergson but also by William James, Samuel Alexander and A. N. Whitehead. And its broad object was to reverse the tradition of epistemological separation (mind and body, cause and effect, one entity distinct from another) in the name of a more fluent and fluid whole universe.

Where Western philosophy has mainly been a philosophy of things; of substances, process philosophy, as the name suggests, argues that existence consists rather in processes, in events and occurrences, in rhythmic fluctuations and modes of change rather than fixed stabilities. The primary realities are not substances but momentary experiences. In other words, process philosophy may be designated as a philosophy which suggests the world is best understood not in terms of nouns but verbs.

This is crucial in Shakespeare not because on some statistical count he works more with verbs than nouns, but because the way he works with all language, as we shall see in more detail in later chapters, is to use it dynamically as if almost everything was of the nature of a fast-released verb rather than an ever-fixed name. He did not bother much with punctuation but wanted one thing to pass into another, with flashes of meaning thrown out even in the passing. It is in that spirit that Hazlitt spoke of Shakespeare's 'magic power over words': 'they come winged at his bidding; and seem to know their places. They are struck out at a heat, on the spur of the occasion.' For Shakespeare, says Hazlitt, 'seems always hurrying from his subject, even while describing it; but the stroke, like the lightning's, is sure as it is sudden' ('On Shakspeare and Milton'). When Romeo heavily requests 'th'exchange of thy love's faithful vow for mine', Juliet replies so swiftly, 'I gave thee mine before thou didst request it', adding in another second, 'And yet I would it were to give again' (*Romeo and Juliet*, 2.1.169–71). 'Give' may be the verb for the noun 'vow', but it is the words 'before' and 'again' that do the real verb-like work in the quick process of Shakespearean time. No wonder Hazlitt loved *Romeo and Juliet*: it was the play closest to the sheer temporal vitality of his *Essay on the Principles of Human Action*.

But there is a second major idea in process philosophy which is also crucial and indeed also consonant with all that goes into Hazlitt's *Essay on the Principles of Human Action*. It is this: that the experiencing thing and the thing experienced are not truly separate, as subject and object, but abstractions from the unity of an occasion or happening. It happens now, it happens between people, the 'it' being the reality of which the people are but part. Afterwards or apart, they, like Agamemnon, recast 'it' in their own terms, at angles of deflection from a reality that is much bigger than themselves. But that, as Hazlitt said, is secondary, because no longer in the living present of the happening. For the new generation of Shakespeareans, the wider and shifting reality of the happening is vital. It means *not* thinking in static blocks, units and divisions – of character *or* story, of past *and* present *and* future all chopped up and distinct, of distinct sensations or faculties such as passion *versus* reason, or forces *either* inside *or* outside 'the self'. For, as I shall continue to show in the chapters that follow, the physical units of Shakespeare's world are porous to the anterior flow of invisible forces and changing rhythms, in a whole which is continually merging together and moving apart in sudden unexpected movements across bounds.

What is more, Shakespeare did have his own sense of process philosophy – not least via his reading of the essays of Montaigne in the translation by John Florio:

> We have no communication with being, for every humane nature is ever in the middle betweene being borne and dying … And if perhaps you fix your thought to take its being, it would be even as if one should go about to graspe the water … Heraclitus averreth that no man ever entered twice one same river … and that one mortall substance could not twise be found in one selfe estate: for by the sodainesse and lightnesse of change sometimes it wasteth, and other times it assembleth; now it comes and now it goes; in such sort, that he who beginneth to be borne never comes to the perfection of being … And nothing remaineth or ever continueth in one state. For to prove it, if we should ever continue one and the same, how is it that now we rejoice at one thing, and now at another? How comes it to passe, we love things contra[dicto]ry? … For time is a fleeting thing, and which appeareth as in a shadow, with the matter ever gliding, always fluent without being stable and permanent.
>
> *Essays*, 2.12, 'An Apology for Raymond Sebond'

In 'the middle' of this flow, Reason has sought solid universals, generalities, permanent laws to hold onto, tying origins to endings. But as Bacon also saw in his *Novum Organum*, too often these reasonings are Idols of the mind, preconceptions of the race so fundamental to our nature and to our very capacity to think as for us not even to be able to think about them, by definition, as illusions. If or when we ever do realize that generalizing reason fails us in the knowledge of life, says Montaigne, we turn to experience instead. And there we are hardly better off in the way of predictability, for so often all we find is a baffling array of particulars instead. As he says in 'Of Experience' (3.13), the consequence we seek to draw from the *likeness* between events is unsure, since they all show *unlikenesses* too. The argument is not even that every occurrence is completely and utterly unique in every aspect, but, more confusedly, this: that as no event, and no form or face, entirely resembles another, so do they not entirely differ from one another either. Such complex blending and unpredictable combination of life's elements and causes leaves Montaigne to conclude half-ruefully, 'Oh, ingenious mixture of Nature!'

In 'How we weepe and laugh at one selfe-same thing' (1.37) Montaigne explicitly quotes and follows Lucretius:

> It is said that the Sunnes-light is not of one continued piece, but that it so uncessantly and without intermissions doth cast so thicke new raies, one in the necke of another, upon us, that wee cannot perceive the space betweene them.

Similarly, human beings are not one whole continuous thing either, though our normal way of seeing makes us think so. It is that 'space between', often too microscopic or too fleeting for the human eye, that Montaigne and Shakespeare alike want to catch, like a ray of thought within the sunlight. In the stream of life, the mind is not made up of states but of movements: 'Our life is nothing but motion' (3.13). And nothing can be fixed for certain, 'both the judgeing and the judged being in continuall alteration and motion' (2.12).

With Montaigne, there is a mobility in prose equivalent to that found in Shakespeare's poetry. In a world that 'runnes all on wheeles' where 'all things therein move without intermission', the only thing Montaigne has constantly with him is himself and even that only moment by moment:

> I take it in this plight, as it is at the instant I amuse myself about it, I describe not the essence but the passage; not a passage from age to age, or as the people reckon, from seaven yeares to seaven, but from day to day, from minute to minute. My history must be fitted to the present. I may soone change'.

> *Essays*, 3.2, 'Of Repenting'.

The 'essay' is his form for painting not the '*essence*' – not the being of some allegedly fixed identity – but the '*passage*', the becoming, the inconstant and untidy changing of the self in all its individually varying occurrences, its unresolved ideas and seeming contradictions. For an essay does not aim at the conclusive or the definitive in the way of permanent truth; sceptical of the possibility of finality, it allows and rides with whatever it is that happens and occurs within the mind, openly raiding all memories and all histories, all thoughts and all books, in the chance, experimental and expressive present of its writing. For Montaigne, the freewheeling essay is about living in time even in the act of writing, for writing here is not about arranging material in categories and by system, pretending to create fixity. This form of writing has a different, more literary sort of permanence: a written *voice* making tonally available what, in every reading, recovers the living experience of transience again.

That is why Hazlitt himself described Montaigne in *Lectures on the English Comic Writers* (1819) as 'the first who had the courage to say as an author what he felt as a man'. Montaigne opens 'Of Repenting' by saying 'Others fashion man; I repeat him; and represent a particular one, but ill made.' The essay is thus about Montaigne imperfectly feeling his way – even to the point of writing in disconnected clauses, leaving in the gaps, not believing that thought can be delivered all at once and as a whole. And as the essays mount up over 16 years, with all their different occasions and changing thoughts, they are fragments in the gradual accretion of an implicit autobiography – but one assembled as the life itself is: written every now and again from inside an ongoing life, rather than from outside and above it all, in controlled retrospect. If the essays fit together at all, even in their contradictions, they do so only implicitly in the way that the man who writes them may fit together, without himself ever necessarily knowing or creating it.

Yet precisely because of this consciousness of mobility, of the shifting uncertainty of only apparently stable, solid-looking boundaries, there is a second-order movement in Montaigne which is concerned above all with the preservation of the separate early-modern self, retreating into his writing in his study-tower. In 'How one ought to Governe his Will' (3.9) Montaigne speaks in defence of almost artificially pulling back inside himself, away from the dangers of external over-commitment:

> Mine opinion is, that one should lend himselfe to others, and not give himselfe but to himself ... Thou hast businesse enough within thy selfe, therefore stray not abroad: men give themselves to hire. Their faculties are not their own, but theirs to whom they subject themselves ...

Drawing clear boundaries between inside and out, trying to calculate the degree of involvement that would ensure he was lending himself and not giving himself away, using mind in detachment from that power of emotion which puts one in hock to persons or events outside: this is not a dishonourable survival strategy in a man caught, physically and psychologically, in the midst of the French civil wars of religion. 'I see some transforme and transubstantiate themselves into as many new formes and strange beings as they undertake charges'; but I, he says, 'abandon the subject which beginnes to molest me, and before it transport me'. That precautionary 'before' of Montaigne's is not the same as Juliet's generous, giving 'before'. Montaigne would evade the real-life drama of his world. Writing for him goes on in literal and mental retreat, within the bounds of a separate autobiographical self, defending itself.

But for Shakespeare, such second-order defences, though interesting, are just that – second-order. He doesn't have to be just one person, he doesn't even have to write like a person: Emerson said of him in *Representative Men* (1850), 'he was the farthest reach of subtlety compatible with an individual self' (Chapter 5). Nothing distracts Shakespeare from the primary dynamic of life-as-drama. When Lear asks Cordelia what she has to say to win her share of the kingdom, it is one of those moments when, for all the physical boundaries, Shakespeare's people can lose power, even through 'Nothing' – and not just power over others but the inner energy of their own life-forces, dispersed in some wider force-field that a Montaigne would keep out of. It is the most serious version of what happens to the Fool in *Twelfth Night* if he cannot answer back in the quick process of repartee or if answering back can have no effect: 'Unless you laugh and minister occasion to him', taunts Malvolio, 'he is gagged' (1.5.82–3). Being 'put down' is almost literally like dying a little in losing life's strength: 'Now you see, sir, how your fooling grows old, and people dislike it' (1.5.106–7). Energy moves and the surrounding world changes with it.

The Mental Palimpsest

But, it may finally be objected, modern scholarship seems to suggest that there is no 'original text' in Shakespeare. There are now two separately printed versions of *King Lear*, *The History of King Lear* in the Quarto text of 1608 and *The Tragedy of King Lear* in the 1623 Folio. There is the *Hamlet* of the second and better Quarto of 1604 and a later, changed and reduced version, again in the 1623 Folio, while behind both there is a lost revenge-play which survives in the background as an older, cruder and simpler response to the murder of a father. There may be a lost, earlier and longer text of *Macbeth*. And even these differing versions that we do have may be no more than coalescing points along a spectrum of varied revision and performance: there may be no one stable text.

This is not surprising. At almost any moment the language of Shakespeare is so *full* of potential as to be able to take almost any turn before closing down. Banquo says to the witches, 'If you can look into the seeds of time | And say which grain will grow and which will not | Speak then to me' (*Macbeth*, 1.3.56–8). But there are always in Shakespeare's mind millions of these verbal seeds, these nascent hints and thoughts of life – some of which go on to live and grow as people; some to become embodied in events and structures; others to find no niche and die away this time, yet perhaps to get their chance again in a different form in another play. This is what Hazlitt meant by the plays not seeming set and finished but always in mental 'rehearsal' of themselves. As Isabella so remarkably says of Angelo in lines that are vital:

> His act did not o'ertake his bad intent,
> And must be buried but as an intent
> That perished by the way. Thoughts are no subjects;
> Intent but merely thoughts.

> *Measure for Measure*, 5.1.448–51

That tiny felt pause between 'intent' at the end of one line and 'perished' near the beginning of the next, leaves 'intent' for a moment hanging there as bare potential which could live or fade. Which it is will be decided in a second in Shakespeare's mind as set out in the play. For in this pause is a micro-image of what will or will not come to anything, at the macro-level in Shakespeare's plays. In *Creative Evolution* Bergson says that life succeeds by making itself very small, at crucial points of nascent decision. And all the time in Shakespeare one thing happens because a hundred other hinted alternatives do not, and you can feel something of those possible variations momentarily massing as the background to the route that is taken.

It is like all that is tacitly summoned by that little word 'else', slipped in when Macbeth hears that though Banquo is murdered, Fleance has escaped. Banquo's throat is cut, reports one of the murderers:

MACBETH: Thou art the best o'th' cut-throats.
                     Yet
                         he's good
                  That did the like for Fleance. If
                  thou
                         didst it,
                  Thou art the non-pareil.

FIRST MURDERER:	Most royal sir,
	Fleance is scaped.
MACBETH:	Then comes my fit again; I had else
	been perfect

And Macbeth stays for a moment, expanding upon the imagination of a now lost future and the room for life there would have been in it:

> Whole as the marble, founded as the rock,
> As broad and general as the casing air

And then 'else' from one part of the mind must give way to the alternative life now to be followed through in another part. That is to say, 'else', not so much a word you could look up in a dictionary as a mental trigger, becomes 'But now', the shorthand for a different, more claustrophobic mental shape:

> But now I am cabined, cribbed, confined, bound in
> To saucy doubts and fears. But Banquo's safe?
>
> *Macbeth*, 3.4.16–24

That's all that 'safe' can mean now for Macbeth – that Banquo is dead. I am saying that words such as 'else' or 'but' are not really words; they are more like what we might now call synapses, signifying almost physical shifts of mental pathways, moving from parallel lives to different minds. It's like the existence of the old *ur-Hamlet* play, the old primitive brain, a throwback beneath the newer layers of thinking in the protagonist, still wheeling in and out of modern consciousness.

Thus, Shakespeare's is an original text because you can feel how even apparently simple little words such as 'else' or 'but', arising in the midst of a passage of thought, really make a structural difference, as if they were part of an *under-language*. I mean by that a language beneath the macro-level of familiar humanistic descriptions or outcomes such as happy or sad; a quasi-neurological language affecting movements of brain at a level anterior to mental conceptualization but en route to it; a language showing meaning coming into being from deep physical shapings of mentality. You can sense as if for the first time again why the word 'but' had to be invented, in midstream as it were, as a form of revision, and what difference the invention of that tool-word made in our conscious evolution of different levels and directions of mentality. Such turning-points let you see momentarily, beneath the direction that is followed, disappearing traces of the alternative routes not taken this time. With Shakespeare, it is like learning our language again in ways that also give us access to the underlying processes of formation.

That is why when the language in Shakespeare takes a complicated shape across the lines, you know you are in the presence of primary evidence – not paraphrase, but the structuring of the mind itself. You fly blind in Shakespeare: you hear and feel the mental shifts and changes and twists and turns, and you are not told in advance when they are coming or in retrospect what they are called. But you know you have followed some formative evolutionary move. And so, just one example to end on here.

Think of Edgar, in disguise, watching blind Gloucester 'fall' from his non-existent cliff: it could not have killed him, he has only fallen flat on his face. Though modern editions rationalize and familiarize it by calling it simply an 'aside', Edgar says, out loud to no one, what *has* to be an utterance in the world – because of the sheer impact of its reality there:

> And yet I know not how conceit may rob
> The treasury of life, when life itself
> Yields to the theft. Had he been where he thought,
> By this had thought been past.

The Tragedy of King Lear, 4.5.42–5

I can paraphrase this: physically this pratfall could not have killed Gloucester, but, terrifyingly, the sheer inner imagination ('conceit') of falling thousands of feet may have been enough to do so. But I do *not* know all that the telling feel of its *shape* really means:

'Had he been where he *thought*/By this had *thought* been past' [my italics]. I do not know what that recursive loop between the two soundings of the word 'thought' is doing to the very organ of thought itself, though so much of the play turns round on itself, biting its own hand, in that fashion. I only know that this is a language with a punctuation so implicit as to affect cerebration by means deeper than just paraphraseable sense. The realization of what, even unconsciously, thought can do to itself and to its thinker; the coalescing force-field of multiple thought-realities in Gloucester, Edgar, Shakespeare, the reader, the spectator, in and around the moment – all this is something of what is at stake here.

But the knowing comes second, said Macaulay. In his 1825 essay, 'Milton', Macaulay had half-lamented that explaining was all that was done now. If Shakespeare had been asked to write a book *about* the complex motives of human action, said Macaulay, he could not have done it; what he could do was to bring into being the motives themselves in the creation of his plays. Now, Macaulay argued, we know more but create less. Conscious understanding is what comes afterwards. What Shakespeare got right was something close to creation itself.

In the order of life, the first thing is to get the blind feel of the thing happening. William James says we are like bars of iron surrounded by electro-magnetic fields:

It is as if a bar of iron, without touch or sight, with no representative faculty whatever, might nevertheless be strongly endowed with an inner capacity for magnetic feeling; and as if, through the various arousals of its magnetism by magnets coming and going in its neighbourhood, it might be consciously determined to different attitudes and tendencies. Such a bar of iron could never give you an outward description of the agencies that had the power of stirring it so strongly; yet of their presence, and of their significance for its life, it would be intensely aware through every fibre of its being.

The Varieties of Religious Experience (1902), Lecture 3

For there we are, like blind and dumb things, sensing a field of forces and energies passing around us and within us. 'All we know is that there are dead feelings, dead ideas, and cold beliefs, and there are hot and live ones; and when one grows hot and alive within us, everything has to re-crystallize about it' (Lecture 9). When the thoughts that come light up the brain or seem momentarily to change its configuration, then we are in the process of sensing how important they are through this under-language. To modify the metaphor again, Shakespeare is the most electric of writers. It is that form of being, and how to have it, which I wish to know more about in what follows. But in a dynamic world the order of things must follow the order of evolution at least in this: first, recreate the original text, the feeling, the physical mentality – by performance or by quotation – and only then do the thinking off it.

2 Shakespeare's Codes

Getting the order right means beginning at the right place. Then you can leave the thing to work itself out, with your tendance. Sometimes Shakespeare feels he has to be explicit about his own starting points, and it is always useful to us when he does lay out his usually implicit and fast things in (relatively) slow motion. Thus, famously, at the opening of *Henry V* a choric voice calls upon the audience: 'Can this cockpit hold | The vasty fields of France?' Audience members who know their Shakespeare will catch the slight physical pressure of the line-ending coming at the word 'hold' – as though, by one of those secret tiny prompts that Shakespeare loves, to stress the paradox: How can a small space ever contain a large one?

By my words and with your help, is the Chorus' answer:

> Piece out our imperfections with your thoughts.
> Into a thousand pieces divide one man,
> And make imaginary puissance.
> Think when we talk of horses that you see them
> Printing their proud hooves i'th' receiving earth,
> For 'tis your thoughts that now must deck our kings,
> Carry them here and there, jumping o'er times,
> Turning th'accomplishment of many years
> Into an hourglass –
>
> *Henry V*, Prologue, 23–31

Yet for all this apologetic pleading of the Chorus here, at the play's commencement, it is not that the audience's involvement in Shakespeare is merely an optional extra for the rest of the time. In the heat of the plays themselves, that involvement is *tacitly* demanded. Space is compressed – the vast fields within the wooden circle; time is compressed – years within an hourglass; and by a powerfully compressed language the audience itself is mentally pulled in to fill the human gaps.

For Nature in Shakespeare abhors a vacuum. Shakespeare's first rule is: If there is a space, it must be filled – by some bursting word, some feeling, some thought, some body on stage or off. 'Here lay Duncan,' cries Macbeth, 'And his gashed stabs looked like a breach in nature | For ruin's wasteful entrance' (*Macbeth*, 2.3.113–14). 'Confusion', 'ruin' come rushing in, like the words into Shakespeare's brain, filling the spaces, making the links – in an image of Shakespearean creativity on the verge of chaos.

But Shakespeare also loves to create that space, the summoning vacuum, in the first place. Lecturing on *The Tempest* around 1811, Coleridge said that one simple, admirable secret of Shakespeare's art was that 'separate speeches frequently do not appear to have been occasioned by those which preceded them'. Rather, they appear 'to have arisen out of the peculiar character of the speaker'.[1] It is not just *one* speech mechanically following another in linear fashion, but a dialogue between *two* simultaneously different mental centres – *plus* the space thus created in between them. Out of that space, charged with joint meaning, may be generated further thoughts, new characters and newly evolving configurations.

Such a matrix recalls a magical-scientific-poetic world in which not just humans but matter, air and space themselves have sense and appetite. As the Lucretius-influenced Dominican monk, Tomasso Campanella, put it in *De sensu rerum et magia* (1620):

> We can well imagine that … things, in order to occupy that space which is at the basis of being, rush to fill it, almost as if they desired to acquire a new realm and a new existence. We may

conjecture further that since the air hurries to prohibit a vacuum, there is joy felt in filling a void; and that the rush is not so much to prohibit the vacuum as it is to spread out in space; for the love of expanding oneself, multiplying oneself, and living full lives in spacious existence obtains in all things.

It is not bodies that give unity to the world, says Campanella, for bodies are often contraries in struggle, but rather it is space which loves to 'interpose itself even between separate bodies and binds the world together', offering a rich, expansive and yet cohesive sense of existence.[2]

It is that space which finds an opening voice for itself in the Chorus of *Henry V*, functioning as Gower does in *Pericles* 'who stand[s] i' the gaps' between acts and scenes, charting the changes (*Pericles*, Scene 18, 8). But within those gaps, at another level, the language itself begins to act like a Cleopatra in its summoning force:

> From the barge
> A strange invisible perfume hits the sense
> Of the adjacent wharfs. The city cast
> Her people out upon her, and Antony,
> Enthroned i'th' market-place, did sit alone,
> Whistling to th'air, which but for vacancy
> Had gone to gaze on Cleopatra too,
> And made a gap in nature.
>
> *Antony and Cleopatra*, 2.2.218–25

Gaps are impossible: as soon as one threatens to open, something is summoned into place, like imagination filling in for the fields of Agincourt. 'Piece out our imperfections with your thoughts.' At such points it is not perfect scenery that is wanted, whatever the resources of the modern theatre, but rather an equivalent of that 'strange invisible perfume' rebounding like a sound-wave in the brain. 'O, it came o'er my ear like the sweet sound | That breathes upon a bank of violets | Stealing and giving odour' (*Twelfth Night*, 1.1.5–7). This joy in filling space, this love of expansion is the celebratory life-force which made Samuel Johnson believe that comedy was the genre most naturally congenial to Shakespeare. For it is only when that primary joy and love are baulked, and the space for them restricted, that pain comes into Shakespeare's world. 'I have gained my experience', claims the melancholy Jaques, though his extensive travels among mankind have never offered him any corresponding largeness of spirit. And to this Rosalind magnificently retorts, 'And your experience makes you sad. I had rather have a fool to make me merry than experience to make me sad', adding merrily enough to prove her point, '– and to travel for it too!' (*As You Like It*, 4.1.24–7). Shakespearean comedy so often makes you quickly happy, makes you believe in happiness, in resisting sadness or in transforming it. 'When I said I would die a bachelor, I did not think I should live till I were married', cries Benedick, in the name of something more vital and excited than straight-laced self-consistency: 'The world must be peopled' (*Much Ado About Nothing*, 2.3.229–31).

All this vitality starts from an empty stage, and the spaces between the bodies that increasingly come upon it. The frank 'imperfection' of the bare minimum is what the director Peter Brook (1966) called (in a book of the same name) 'the empty space' – to remind us that Shakespeare's means of communication is not simply naturalistic or imitative. *Think!* cries that solitary opening voice in *Henry V*:

> Think when we talk of horses that you see them
> Printing their proud hooves i'th'receiving earth.

Only on a bare stage is it utterly clear that what I can *see* is far less than what I begin to *think*, as a result of all that the language *talks of* in between those two. Too much that is material and visible gets in the way of thought's 'piecing it out' – thought's wonderful completing of the thing, by one piece or one sense compensating for another. Alberti said in *De Statua* (1450) that the first images were made when people discovered by accident, in some tree trunk or lump of earth, certain contours that needed only a slight alteration to look strikingly like some natural object – an addition or subtraction to complete what was lacking. Antony saw shapes in clouds that resembled dragon, bear or lion, citadel, rock, tree or mountain (*Antony and Cleopatra*, 4.15.2–7). We need only the exciting economy of equivalent clues or prompts, like sketches. And then in *Henry V* we can momentarily *feel*, even through the imagined earth in that soft word '*receiving*', the firm and heavy print of the horses' '*proud* hooves'. When Hamlet suddenly says he thinks he sees his father, and a startled Horatio asks, 'Where, my lord?', Hamlet replies: 'In my mind's eye, Horatio' (*Hamlet*, 1.2.184). It is the same dynamic that Ruskin was to find in the painter Turner, that quintessential sketcher even in oil, who makes you see that art *cannot* simply imitate nature *and* that there is a virtue in that imperfection:

> Thus, in the case of all sketches, etchings, unfinished engravings, etc., no one ever supposes them to be imitations. Black outlines on white paper cannot produce a deceptive resemblance of anything; and the mind, understanding at once that it is to depend on its own powers for great part of its pleasure, sets itself so actively to the task that it can completely enjoy the rudest outline in which meaning exists. Now when it is once in this temper, the artist is infinitely to be blamed who insults it by putting anything into his work which is not suggestive: having summoned the imaginative power, he must turn it to account and keep it employed, or it will turn against him in indignation. Whatever he does merely to realize and substantiate an idea is impertinent; he is like a dull story-teller, dwelling on points which the hearer anticipates or disregards. The imagination will say to him: I knew all that before; I don't want to be told that. Go on; or be silent, and let me go on my own way. I can tell the story better than you.
>
> *The Stones of Venice*, vol. 3 (1853), Chapter 4, para 23

Too much slow and solemn naturalism gets in the way: we need the creative impatience of speed, felt space, shorthand language-code, and sketch. In Shakespeare, remarkably, thinking means momentarily seeing the invisible, there on the stage: 'In my mind's eye'.

Cross-senses

In the continuing to-and-fro transition between an oral and a print culture in the Elizabethan age, the suddenly demanded shifts from eye to ear, from words to imagination, as we witness the action on stage, are just as powerful as was the shift the other way from voice to script. As an anonymous writer puts it in a commonplace book from the 1630s, on the birth of 'the rich art of writing':

> when men
> Spake without voices, the deputed pen
> Did ye tongue['s] office, and ye ey turnd eare
> To ye dead voice and p[ro]perly did heare,
> It maz'd ye world, the Interp'ter of thought
> Should have another channel than ye throate.[3]

Whichever way you come at it – reading a Shakespeare play or seeing it – there is a constant movement of the brain from one of its senses to another, the understanding working first through one 'channel', then trying its way via another, and so on. The physical abruptly turns mental in the theatre, and the distance from the stage suddenly closes as the language zooms the audience in. Even in silent reading, the text feels like a musical score, with lines as thought's voices and performance's shapes. The text is truly a medium here, between page and stage, or stage and audience, vibrating all along the spectrum between the physical and mental. This is no place for what Hamlet hates in his mother: 'Eyes without feeling, feeling without sight, | Ears without hands or eyes' (*Hamlet*, 3.4.78–9).

Wherever we are, we can almost literally see thinking as *happening* in Shakespeare. Thinking becomes almost visible, like an event, present both on the stage and between the stage and audience. Macbeth 'clutches' at the dagger that he sees before him, yet he can't grasp it or feel it. If it's not there, it must be – he then thinks by a quick shift of sense – 'a dagger of the mind' (*Macbeth*, 2.1.38). No wonder, with such experience of shifting senses and media, Shakespeare was a master of metaphor. For 'a dagger of the mind' marks a movement central to the evolutionary principle of metaphor – translating the ostensibly physical into the realm of the inferred psychological and thus giving the mental a language. At this moment the mind is suddenly discovered even by itself, in front of its own eyes, as it were, to wonder at its own unconscious powers. 'How is't with me, when every noise appals me? | What hands are here?' (*Macbeth*, 2.2.61–2). In this language, nothing is taken for granted and nothing is already known. With Shakespeare, whatever it is, it is always as though for the first time again. Mind, like character itself, is not there to begin with in Shakespeare; it is dramatically *thought into being* on the stage. It is that way round: the thought suddenly creating consciousness – the consciousness of what it is that is thinking it. It is not the old classical principle of *operari sequitur esse* – such that 'being' comes first and then 'function' follows from it. It is not that characters can enter fully-formed. Rather, the right order with Shakespeare is that of evolutionary theory and of process philosophy – that being follows from function and is itself created by what can be done. In a sort of mental loop, the mind of a Lear or a Macbeth is terrified to see what events show he has become.

I want to look, a little bit longer, at how thinking is visibly present in Shakespeare as an action with a space of its own on stage. For Shakespeare reveals a form of thinking which is not usually that of some Rodin statue, fingers long-pressed to pondering brow, the faculty of reason working away steadily and continuously in some private room inside the house of the mind. Even Hamlet's soliloquies are far jumpier than that. Rather, thinking is first of all a dramatic and sporadic flash in Shakespeare, then a suddenly realized evolution of another level of being, called into place by gaps in the experience of reality.

Here is a second example of Shakespeare in slower motion than usual. When Cressida leaves Troy and Troilus and, for all her vows, inclines to Diomedes the Greek, it's all over for Troilus. 'All's done, my lord,' says Ulysses. 'It is,' Troilus acknowledges, and yet he still stands staring at the spot where he has just seen Cressida betray him. 'Why stay we then?' says Ulysses again.

We stay because there are some *thoughts* left there, invisibly, that Cressida seems to have abandoned to that now empty place. And in Shakespearean physics, the law is that *some* body has to pick them up and make them speak and be seen. Thought cries out for some receiver, some channel for itself. 'Was Cressid here?' cries Troilus in this after-vacancy (*Troilus and Cressida*, 5.2.127).

> This she? No, this is Diomed's Cressida.
> If beauty have a soul, this is not she.
> If souls guide vows, if vows be sanctimonies,
> If sanctimony be the gods' delight,
> If there be rule in unity itself,
> This is not she.
>
> *Troilus and Cressida*, 5.2.140–5

If, if, if, if, this, this, this, this; no, not, not: these minimal shorthand words are like the surrounding parameters of the syntax; they are the skeletal outlines of that blank space well-nigh *without* words that Troilus' thought has now to try to fill *with* them. Crucially, then, for a split-second in Shakespeare you feel you can almost separate the syntactic structures from the semantic sense – distinguishing the non-verbal mental tracks from the words and sentences they will almost instantaneously be translated into – just before the two come together again in one.[4] 'This', repeatedly, is the place where she was, and the thought of her he looks at, and also the very shape of his mental dilemma. 'She' surely is not *both* Troilus' Cressida *and* Diomedes' Cressida. For in this suspended and extended moment he cannot believe that the one has simply succeeded the other, linearly, as though human beings were no more than creatures of occasion in time. How can she be two people? Yet how can she be one?

> This is, and is not, Cressid.
> Within my soul there doth conduce a fight
> Of this strange nature, that a thing inseparate
> Divides more wider than the sky and earth;
> And yet the spacious breadth of this division
> Admits no orifex for a point as subtle
> As Ariachne's broken woof to enter.
>
> *Troilus and Cressida*, 5.2.149–55

There is between these two Cressids the widest of all gaps and yet, equally, no one point – not even the tiniest eye of an needle – at which to locate it. How did it happen? Where has the meaning gone? Was it just of my thinking, like Macbeth's dagger, a Cressida of the mind, not she? 'What's aught but as 'tis valued?' (*Troilus and Cressida*, 2.2.51).

Thought here stands in the place of a person who may or may not have existed, the shadow of Cressida like the ghost of Banquo. What Troilus, belated in his shock, really wants to locate is that lost point of transition when Cressida somehow changed. That is why it has to be Thought – because its subject cannot be seen, or grasped, or found materially existent. And mind itself in Shakespeare, as here in Troilus, is not a substance; it is what is belatedly called into being in the space between things – in that impossible yet vitally missing space in between Cressida past and present. Yet as one philosopher central to our story has put it, 'The attempt at introspective analysis in these cases is in fact like … trying to turn up the gas quickly enough to see how the darkness looks':

There is not a conjunction or a preposition, and hardly an adverbial phrase, syntactic form, or inflection of voice, in human speech, that does not express some shading or other of relation which we at some moment actually feel to exist between the larger objects of our thought … The relations are numerous, and no existing language is capable of doing justice to all the shades.

We ought to say a feeling of *and*, a feeling of *if*, a feeling of *but*, and a feeling of *by*, quite as readily as we say a feeling of *blue* or a feeling of *cold*. Yet we do not: so inveterate has our habit become of recognizing the existence of the substantive parts alone, that language almost refuses to lend itself to any other use.

William James, The Principles of Psychology (1890), Chapter 9

To William James, the mind's normal grammar barely reflects the brain's actual movements. Its grammar is like the travesty of crude paraphrase: it offers great obvious blocks of time (past, present, future) and of separate, substantive feelings coming to the surface (hot, cold, sorrow, joy, anger), while omitting the continuous process that goes on in subtle shadings between those reifications. Even where it does offer conjunctions, the mind has no language for what those shaping connectives really mean as feeling, as inarticulate experience intrinsic to its own deeper workings.

But, perhaps uniquely, Shakespeare's language is *not* like that, and does not merely use the solid building-bricks of names and nouns or the dry, residual clarity of informative propositions. Rather, it takes us down into the brain's deep in-between formative places, even while replicating the experience of their still being barely catchable. Although all Troilus' speech is a struggle for the right terms of conjunction between Cressida now and Cressida before, even in Troilus's stammering failure Shakespeare is capable of doing justice to the feeling of *if* or *this* or *not* or *and*. 'I do not like "But yet",' cries Cleopatra: '"But yet" is as a gaoler to bring forth | Some monstrous malefactor' (*Antony and Cleopatra*, 2.5.51–3). But Touchstone likes an 'if': for in the quarrel that goes 'If you said so, then I said so', 'Your "if" is the only peacemaker;

much virtue in "if"' (*As You Like It*, 5.4.98–101). Yet what Hamlet suggests, as George T. Wright puts it, 'is that the conjunctions on which life depends, on which this world's customs and institutions are founded, cannot be trusted'[5]: 'God hath given you one face and you make yourselves another', 'The body is with the King, but the King is not with the body (*Hamlet*, 3.2.146–7; 4.2.26–7).

Yet Shakespeare's conjunctions are at their most powerful when tacit, when given not so much a word as a minutely pausing place within the rhythm of the world. That tiny place is created by the line-endings, the crucially implicit syntactic tool that Shakespeare finds when a sentence is too full to be contained *in* the line but has to go *across* it and may even have to end mid-line. This is poetry not first of all as fine language but as an act of realignment. As soon as the original score is performed on stage, the brain has to give up on seeing these transitions but it may just about hear and sense them. For these transitions catch the passing feelings of a thought even in the midst of its own grammatical formulation:

> Within my soul there doth conduce a fight
> Of this strange nature: that a thing inseparate
> Divides more wider than the sky and earth;
> And yet ...

Thus in this complex nesting of clauses and lines of thought, what makes sense is not just the substantive-blocks going on serially *along the lines* in normally comprehensible time: 'that a thing divides more wider than ...'. There is also, en route to sense, the interstitial electrical movement *between and across and down the lines*, registered just a split second *after* it has happened: 'A thing *inseparate* | *Divides*' [my italics]. There, in that passing mid-feeling of implicit paradox, the line-ending itself, like the mid-line stop, may be the secret 'orifex for a point as subtle'. It is a counterpoint which reproduces to the eye a map of the brain's movement, even as the ear follows the ongoing physical sense, in that strange mixture of permanent text and transient performance in Shakespeare. The original text is like a human life-code, a DNA for coming-to-life in performance.

In Lucretius's universe, atoms should all travel in straight lines of force downwards through empty space by virtue of their own weight. Yet if this were so, says Lucretius, they would never collide and would never form those combinations with each other that set the world going in the ongoing generation of diversity. Actually, he argues, at indeterminate times and places, the atoms swerve ever so slightly from their regular course, and that slight but vital shift from the straight line, crucial to creation, he calls the 'clinamen'. I am saying that in Shakespeare's mental world there is an equivalent to the physics of the hypothetical clinamen. Prosaically, Pericles could say to his newly found daughter, for example: 'Thou that wast born at sea, buried at Tharsus, and found at sea again' – in a straight list of three successive clauses and linear movements. In fact, Shakespeare's poetic code shifts and shapes it like this:

> O, come hither,
> Thou that begett'st him that did thee beget;
> Thou that wast born at sea, buried at Tharsus,
> And found at sea again!

Pericles, 21.182–5

Of course, Shakespeare wants 'O, come hither' to hang at the end of the line, belated and in appeal – like his saying, a little earlier, 'I will believe thee' (111), not placed assertively at the beginning of a line but much more haltingly managed as he tries to take in what has seemed beyond all hope. Even more, Shakespeare wants 'Thou that begett'st him that did thee beget' to be contained-to-bursting in one line that however much it seems to read forward left to right, actually turns round upon itself, the life-flow father-to-daughter becoming daughter-to-father instead. But, above all, Shakespeare wants that final mental and linear shift onto 'And found at sea again'. It is not a straightforward shape but a twist, a tonal change in level for all the earlier direction of the line of thought, a totally unexpected personal turnaround after the usual beat of things. It is also something that comes very, very late in the day. And so the whole movement across the line-endings gives particular expression to the words 'found' and 'again' until they become here the very feel of all that the late plays stand for.

There is a template hidden behind all this, compressed in the later plays, but sometimes revealed more extensively in the earlier ones. Thus in the first instance in Shakespeare, lineation arises most powerfully out of dialogue, as itself a layer parallel to rhyme. In the simple opening mathematics of evens and odds in *A Midsummer Night's Dream*, for instance, there are two similar girls but one lover, who, of course, loves the wrong girl:

> HERMIA: I frown upon him, yet he loves me still!
> HELENA: O that your frowns would teach my
> smiles such skill!
> HERMIA: I give him curses, yet he gives me love.
> HELENA: O that my prayers might such affection
> move!
> HERMIA: The more I hate, the more he follows me.
> HELENA: The more I love, the more he hateth me.
> HERMIA: His folly, Helen, is no fault of mine.
> HELENA: None but your beauty; would that fault
> were mine!
>
> *A Midsummer Night's Dream*, 1.1.194–201

Working off parallel symmetries, the economical principle of structure is that lines can subdivide into two parts internally to themselves ('I give him *curses*, yet he gives me *love*') or externally between two people on different lines ('The more *I hate* ... The more *I love*'), or, indeed, both beautifully together [my italics]. Shakespeare loves that Bach-like economy, that adaptive capacity for further self-generating complexity both along and down the lines, at different levels, in varying senses and sizes. It is partly what Montaigne describes in his essay 'Of Experience' when he speaks of words being batted back and forth like balls between the two protagonists, belonging half to the serving speaker and half to the listening receiver, as in a tennis match. But it is also partly like the work of atoms or cells, bouncing off each other, combining and recombining 'the more, the more'.

The next step is that what goes on in the dialogue between *two* can then go on enfolded more densely in the longer single speech of *one*. If you read one of the sources for *Twelfth Night*, Barnabe Riche's story 'Of Apolonius and Silla', you almost feel that you can tell the original raw moment when, technically, Shakespeare would become most interested. It is when it is no longer a simple matter of one indignant speech by one character serially followed by another from the separate point of view of a second – but rather this, from the Viola figure speaking to the wronged prototype of Olivia, where both are innocently suffering at the hands of the other at the self-same time, and suddenly the Viola figure realizes it:

> I knowe not, madame, of whom I might make complaint, whether of your or of my self, or rather of Fortune, whiche hath conducted and brought us both into so great adversitie. I see that you receive great wrong, and I am condemned againste all right; you in peril to abide the bru[i]te of spightfull tongues, and I in daunger to lose the thing that I moste desire ... [6]

There, suddenly, are *two* points of view registered within what is also *one* of them. It is not just a matter of one individual character's sympathy or fair-mindedness, but more tensely, for Shakespeare, a paradox in the very structure of mental development: the paradox of seeing the two and yet being only one. This is even more the case for Viola herself, disguised as the young man Cesario, the hapless go-between for Count Orsino in his suit to Olivia. All the characters and their relationships now begin to be cast as *lines* within the mind of just one such, in soliloquy. Through Shakespeare's creative mathematics, it is here a structure not just of two but of three lines

– of three people and three overlapping relationships, beginning from a question:

> How will this fadge? My *master* loves *her* dearly,
> And *I*, poor monster, fond *as much* on *him*,
> And *she*, mistaken, seems to dote on *me*:

Then immediately, and again from the question, it mutates into two lines multiplied by two, dividing Viola between man and woman both inside and out:

> What will become of this? As I am *man*
> My state is desperate for my *master's* love:
> As I am *woman* (now alas the day!)
> What thriftless sighs shall poor *Olivia* breathe?
>
> Twelfth Night, 2.2.33–9 [my italics]

And then finally the 'how will *this* fadge?' and the 'what will become of *this*?', at the commencement of each run, come together as the all-too-much of:

> O *time, thou* must untangle *this*, not *I*.
> *It* is too hard a knot for *me* t'untie.
>
> 40–1 [my italics]

As in *A Midsummer Night's Dream* or *As You Like It*, from a point just outside it all there is a structural sympathy here. And when that structure is recognized within one who also knows herself to be only a part of it, then it is as if the human mind has suddenly become much larger than it needs to be to accommodate the single viewpoint of its possessor. And yet, that largeness is still contained within a person who feels herself all the smaller as a result. That is to say, Viola can '*not*' be '*I*' in those last two lines, as she has been in the five before, but must give way to '*Time*' instead; for really she was always, admittedly, just '*me*', secreted and overwhelmed. In Shakespeare the meaning of the whole is always hidden within its own midst, in some disguise. That is why it cannot be that Viola is simply offering up a soliloquy of summarized information for the audience: rather, still within it all, she is reading her own situation, using the lines syntactically to help her to work through the situation by division and then recapitulation, as though they were brain print-outs that she can examine. She is as much hearing the report of her own thinking as giving it: it loops back into her mind, in search of repair mechanisms for the situation.

This sort of internal notation, along and down the lines, is one possibility for us too, in tracing and following Shakespearean thinking in praxis. Instead of the slow over-elaborate language of explanation, we could try to talk in this electric braille, without using any language but Shakespeare's own – picking out these shorthand words of inner dialogue and underlying structure by fast intuition, as I have done above in italics. The quasi-syntactic sequence *her*, *I*, *him*, *she*, *me* lights up the brain with the realization of the full meaning of 'as much', each loving as much and as hopelessly as the other – just as, comically, the letters MOAI light up Malvolio in *Twelfth Night*. It would not be hard to design a software program for actors and students in which, text scrolling down the screen in front of them, they could intuitively highlight the verbal hotspots and connect their linkages down the lines, following the implicit thought through, to produce a sort of diagram of a mini-brain by the end. It would make for something such as Hardy saw in his neo-Darwinist poem of inheritance, 'The Pedigree'. When staring at the Hardy family tree in front of his eyes, he finds that its branches suddenly turn into a kind of neurological mirror of what lies behind those eyes: 'And then did I divine | That every heave and coil and move I made | Within my brain, and in my mood and speech, | Was in the glass portrayed ...' But where Hardy fears that even his apparently spontaneous choices are governed by a form of genetic determinism, in Shakespeare it is the opposite. It is rather that creative freedom itself has underlying laws and structures.

At any rate, the lineation which begins as clarification of the brainwaves amid confusion (he/she; love/hate on distinct lines) goes on in Shakespeare to form a half-disguised language-within-language, a coded pattern or under-language within itself. So it is here, when, as the life of Macbeth drains out of himself, he speaks of his decay:

> And that which should accompany old age,
> As honour, love, obedience, troops of friends,
> I must not look to have; but in their stead,
> Curses, not loud but deep, mouth-honour, breath
> Which the poor heart would fain deny, and dare not.
>
> *Macbeth*, 5.3.26–30

It now does, emotionally, what otherwise it merely says: it makes the list in line 29 ('Curses not loud but deep …') truly '*in the stead*' (line 28) of the list in line 27 ('As honour, love, obedience …') – in terrible contrast between what '*should* accompany' and what actually now does. And line 27 comes first, ahead of 29, because for a moment the lines are themselves two different possible Macbeths in parallel universes, and 27 is the ghost that gives meaning to its later replacement-self in 29, even by its taking meaning away. In Shakespeare, moreover, 'nothing *is* but what *is not*', and what you lose has to be felt as *there* in the first place, before being taken away again in the second. That is why the main verb in the first half of the speech – 'I must not look to have' – comes strandedly *after* and not before its objects, still yearning for a future that has turned past without ever being present. 'I must not look to have | honour, love, obedience, troops of friends' would be more like information only, the line-ending almost literally straightforward; it would not be like having to say a long drawn-out goodbye to all these things just after you have had to feel them again. Shakespeare first uses lines to sort out the mind, to put it into the separate parts it can register; but then he finds he has simultaneously also created the spaces in between them, full of the underlying meaning. And across those spaces the words on different mental lines are beginning to make neurological links and shapes and patterns between themselves, like the very model of a brain caught on the page and coming to life.

Again, we can see something more of what is at stake in these inter-linear moments by taking a third look at a larger, slow-motion format. In the shifting geographical movements of *Pericles*, as I have already said, the poet Gower is offered as a full-scale figure of transition between the acts. Regularly he introduces a dumb show of the principal actors as a sort of rehearsal or pre-echo or neo-Platonic formal sketch-plan, before letting us settle back down into the full flesh-and-blood scene on earth again:

> Well sailing ships and bounteous winds have brought
> This king to Tharsus – think his pilot thought;
> So with his steerage shall your thoughts go on –
> To fetch his daughter home, who first is gone.
> Like motes and shadows see them move a while;
> Your ears unto your eyes I'll reconcile.

> *Dumb show*
> *Enter Pericles at one door, with all his train; Cleon and Dionyza at the other. Cleon shows Pericles the tomb; whereat Pericles makes lamentation, puts on sackcloth, and in a mighty passion departs, followed by his train.*

Scene 18, 17–22

Here are two characteristic moves unusually sketched out ahead of any more finished establishment: one is for the audience, who are collaboratively to make thought itself into Pericles' pilot across the sea; the other is for Pericles, to provide a false background in the supposed death of Marina for what is to come about later. But then, after the dumb show, eye and ear, x-ray and face, shadow and sub-stance, template and human action – here momentarily held apart – will all come back together again as reality's one. To see the two both apart and together is the fascination, as though it were a late-play experiment in the composition of reality. It works for once just

horizontally, not, as normal in Shakespeare, horizontally and verti-
cally fused together. It is the old-fashioned device of the dumb
show, yet here it is transformed into a radical experiment.

What I am saying is that long before the explicit experimentation
of the late plays, there are equivalent in-between moments of mental transition, as between ear and eye, which are hidden in small,
swift nano-seconds of the drama. Cassius, for example, tries to tell
Brutus that he does not really know himself: 'Tell me, good Brutus,
can you see your face?' Brutus replies:

> No, Cassius, for the eye sees not itself
> But by reflection, by some other things.

Julius Caesar, 1.2.54–5

This is no more or less than typical of Shakespeare's sheer power of
lineation. For a moment, the statement is absolute up to the line-
ending: 'the eye sees not itself'. 'If you saw yourself with your eyes',
says Celia to Orlando in *As You Like It*, (1.2.164). That is the first
thought. Then across the line what was absolute is now revealed as
turned relative – 'the eye sees not itself | But by reflection' – and a
second thought ('But by reflection') is added to the first so seam-
lessly as hardly to have ever seemed separate from it in the evolution
of the idea. At the risk of a picky minuteness, we can halt this aural
process, with the eye, at the line-ending; and, then again, across the
silent line-ending, we can see in the dumb gap between the one line
and the other what Gower called the atomic 'motes and shadows' of
the thought, even as they are taking on further substance.

These are not *really* small matters; rather, they are big matters,
only they are happening at life's speed. For 'the eye sees not itself' is
itself a little secret clue as to how the characters, like the actors
themselves, have only 'parts' in the play and do not see the whole
text in which they belong – even when, like Viola, they are at the
very centre of it. So, in *Pericles* again, there is a nice explicit moment
when Simonides, king of Pentapolis, is secretly pleased that his
daughter, Thaisa, has fallen in love with Pericles despite her father's

ostensible objection. For actually her choice agrees with his – it is like a bare-bones rehearsal for Prospero and Miranda in *The Tempest*:

> She tells me here she'll wed the stranger knight,
> Or never more to view nor day nor night.
> I like that well. Nay how absolute she's in't,
> Not minding whether I dislike or no!
> Mistress, 'tis well, I do commend your choice.
>
> *Pericles*, Scene 9, 14–18

Like Simonides, here poised between saying 'she' and 'you', Shakespeare loves that double perspective when what is no more than a relative part becomes for a time autonomous, absolute to itself – just as, in small, a line may stand out for a second from its relation to the sentence into which it finally is absorbed. Thus, the code which is made explicit through Simonides, in a minor part of one play, is the implicit dynamic in suddenly more important parts of other plays: so it is with the drunken Barnardine in *Measure for Measure* stubbornly refusing to be executed for the sake of the wider plot, or the ever-dutiful Imogen in *Cymbeline* finding herself abruptly telling her Roman master that his life 'must shuffle for itself' because she senses something even more imperative now than normal duty (5.6.105). These characters at these moments insist that the whole must be made bigger, to allow such things. And the whole itself, responding like Simonides, secretly needs these ostensibly resistant absolutes in the parts in order to re-form all its relations.

Speed in Shakespeare does not make big matters small, just excitingly brief. The proof of this is the sudden flash of feeling that Shakespeare can yield in us, as though such emotion were the invisible sign of something more important than there is cognitive time for. Some characters, it is true, do want a thinly continuous present-time to dissolve feeling and meaning. Ulysses wanted Troilus simply to move on, and it was Ulysses, significantly, who was insistent to Achilles that everything, even reputation, was measured by its present standing. Lady Macbeth complains to her husband to have 'done':

> How now, my lord, why do you keep alone,
> Of sorriest fancies your companions making,
> Using those thoughts which should indeed have died
> With them they think on?
>
> *Macbeth*, 3.2.10–13

But essentially in Shakespeare the relation of 'thoughts' to the things or the persons 'they think on' is never as simply coincident – and deathly – as Lady Macbeth would have it: there is always a sort of 'clinamen', an inherent living time-lag between the world and our consciousness. What Shakespeare characteristically does, without being disloyal to the dramatic feeling of on-rushing presentness, is to make the transience and the brevity *electric* in their human after-effect – communicative of thoughts huddled tight within split-second feeling, for want of a larger space or time for themselves. Hence, even in Lady Macbeth's attempted write-off of meaning, there is the explosive force from the slip of that word 'died', rather than merely 'ended', left for a second at the line-close. The ostensibly metaphorical 'died' really comes, of course, from the literal murder of both Duncan and Banquo, without the Macbeths having killed off the still-spreading thought of those two.

Thus, along his lines, the human route for Shakespeare involves a momentary stay against time, in the midst of having still physically to go with it. So it is with Hermione, speaking of the loss of Leontes' love to Leontes himself, as he madly threatens her with death for adultery:

> Sir, spare your threats:
> The bug which you would fright me with, I seek.
> To me can life be no commodity.
> The crown and comfort of my life, your favour,

> I do give lost, for I do feel it gone,
> But know not how it went
>
> *The Winter's Tale*, 3.2.90–5

For a felt second between the end of one line – 'for I do feel it gone' – and the beginning of the next – 'But know not how it went' – there is a momentary inward flashback, holding the mental space that Hermione occupies, even as her world goes on without her. For humans, there has to be space, time, room for such a word or such a feeling in the telegraphese of 'feel-it-gone', but 'know-not-how-it-went' – unless one has become like Macbeth, emptily hearing of the death of his wife. Within its confinements, the human script needs its pauses, needs the room, however minute and passing, for particular individual emphases, for varying physico-emotional rhythms, when such as Claudius and Gertrude can say to Hamlet that a father's death is merely 'common'. 'Why seems it so *particular* with thee?' (*Hamlet*, 1.2.75) [my italics]. The characters, and the actors who recreate them, have to make or find time within the script allowed to them, to give their utterances an autonomous existence in the world. As George T. Wright puts it, 'The sentence and the line, like human personalities, may meet in inexhaustible combinations, never immediately repeating exactly the same rhythms or the same larger units. The line becomes a miniature of the infinitely various and variously polarized larger world.'[7] 'The bug which you would fright me with,' Hermione says, 'I seek': those two simple words, occupying so little space, nonetheless *reverse* the line, changing its whole particular rhythmic character from that of Leontes to that of Hermione, and securing her existence in the play's space-time. That sort of formulation could come out of almost any sixteenth-century book of rhetoric, but here it is as though Shakespeare spontaneously reinvents rhetoric as natural speech in the process of taking form.

All this means that where normally human beings want to think of *one* thing at a time in *one* sense, you begin to be more like Shakespeare when you think of *two* – and then some. This section is called 'Cross-senses' because it has been about how in Shakespeare, to find its way to meaning, the brain must adaptively shift itself from one sense to another, from one plane or pathway to another. It must work from eye to ear, from ear to eye, between line and sentence, via metaphor, through rhythm, from linear movement to sub-linear structurings. So it is with poor Phoebe stunned before the disguised Rosalind: 'and faster than his tongue | Did make offence, his eye did heal it up' (*As You Like It*, 3.5.116–17); or likewise with Olivia caught between at once seeing and hearing Cesario: 'O what a deal of scorn looks beautiful | In the contempt and anger of his lip!' (*Twelfth Night*, 3.1.143–4). But to try to clinch the importance of this law of shifting senses, here is a final slow-motion example of what this means for us ordinary thinkers – this time not taken from Shakespeare himself.

The nineteenth-century Wessex poet beloved of Hardy, William Barnes, is a would-be throw-back to the verbal creativity of Shakespeare's age. But where Shakespeare richly mixes up Saxon and Latinate layers in his fluid compound vocabulary, Barnes feels that, even belatedly, he must seek to rescue English from an overly Latinate abstraction, by concentrating on the more directly physical mentality of a near-lost Dorset dialect. He thus preferred 'I will not be put upon' to 'I will not be imposed upon', 'I looked out var ye' to 'I expected you', 'I zet myself agien it' to 'I opposed it'. A reader could still feel, in the first of each set, the metaphorical evolution of the phrasing emergent from its physical origins of sense. It is in poems such as 'Tokens' that this thickened vocabulary, rooted in place, is fully realized:

> Green mwold in zummer bars do show
> That they've a-dripp'd in winter wet;
> The hoof-worn ring o' groun' below
> The tree, do tell o' storms or het;
> The trees in rank along a ledge
> Do show where woonce did bloom a hedge;
> An' where the vurrow-marks do stripe

The down, the wheet woonce rustled ripe.
Each mark ov things a-gone vrom view –
To eyezight's woone, to soulzight two.

It is not only that the sound of the local place is here connected with its sights, but there is also, within the sight of what *is* there, the imaginative thought of what is not there but has been. That is the soul-sight which is Shakespeare's minimum requirement: that we must see two things, two levels, and work in at least two senses, at once, within a language that can show it happening. Where Barnes does it by memory, Shakespeare did it more immediately by drama. It was a hugely challenging evolutionary leap of mind.

Scanners

But it was a mental leap concealed within the ongoing physical flow of things, soul-sight hidden within eye-sight, thought kept inside the medium of life and time. There is this strangely fluid, sliding sensation in Shakespeare when going along the line suddenly turns into a shift of direction or a change of level only registered the second *after* it has happened, and still left behind.

This happens even as Lear is blustering out his threats before his daughters:

> No, you unnatural hags,
> I will have such revenges on you both
> That all the world shall – I will do such things –
> What they are, yet I know not; but they shall be
> The terrors of the earth. You think I'll weep:
> No, I'll not weep. I have full cause of weeping,
> But this heart shall break into a hundred thousand flaws
> Or ere I'll weep – O Fool, I shall go mad!
>
> *The Tragedy of King Lear*, 2.2.452–9

Take the line 'What they are, yet I know not; but they shall be': the comma after 'are' comes from the second quarto, whereas in folio it is after 'yet', and in the first quarto there is none at all. We know from the only extant manuscript written in Shakespeare's hand – a passage from *Sir Thomas More* – that Shakespeare was extraordinarily light on punctuation, often used line-endings and line-beginnings instead, and sought to notate in the encoded score of his draft only the flowing pace and quasi-musical emphases which he heard for his actors in the hasty physical course of his writing.[8] Modern editors are helpful in their clarification by punctuation, but are also necessarily misleading even in that. Even the editors of the First Folio added or deleted commas, created semi-colons or parentheses. Yet actually it is closer to Shakespeare's mentality to register the minute differences – 'what they are yet, I know not', 'what they are, yet I know not' – by using the line as one for surfing along without any punctuation at all: 'what they are yet I know not but they shall be'. This leaves the speaker working along the line immersed and blind, sensitive to hear and catch the changes in the very midst of his or her own utterance of them, through the sliding movement of time itself. It makes the punctuation internal, cerebral. Within the stream of consciousness, said William James, it is very difficult to catch movements which are in fluent passage of transition:

If they are but flights to a conclusion, stopping them to look at them before the conclusion is reached is really annihilating them. Whilst if we wait till the conclusion is reached, it so exceeds them in vigor and stability that it quite eclipses and swallows them up in its glare. Let anyone try to cut a thought across in the middle and get a look at its section ... The rush of the thought is so headlong that it almost brings us up at the conclusion before we can arrest it. Or if our purpose is nimble enough and we do arrest it, it ceases forthwith to be itself. As a snow-flake crystal caught in the warm hand is no longer a crystal but a drop, so, instead of catching the feeling of relation moving to its term, we find we have caught some substantive thing statically taken.

Psychology: Briefer Course (1892), Chapter 11

This is where Shakespeare loves to be: in the dense fluid process of human beings caught in life-in-time. It demands a particular kind of thinking, thickened even in the midst of its passing elusiveness, as if we were creatures definitely *in* time but not wholly *of* it – like Cleopatra's Antony whose delights, in another of those secret Shakespearean clues, 'Were dolphin-like; they showed his back above | The element they lived in' (*Antony and Cleopatra*, 5.2.88–9).

See again Lear's speech of impotent threatening. Amid the approaching sounds of storm and thunder, which are stage directions to be fitted in somewhere, editors cannot be wholly clear as to the exact lineation of the phrases after 'You think I'll weep' (which comes at the end of a line in all texts):

1. no, I'll not weep
2. I have full cause of weeping
3. but this heart
4. shall break into a hundred thousand flaws
5. or ere I'll weep.

Lines 1 and 2 can be printed as one line or on separate lines; but 2 and 3 equally so; with knock-on effects upon 3 and 4 in both cases. Thus: 'No I'll not weep [*Storm within*] | I have full cause of weeping, but this heart | Shall break . . . (Quarto); or: 'No I'll not weep, I have full cause of weeping | [*Storm and Tempest*] | But this heart shall break into a hundred thousand flaws | Or ere . . .' (Folio). It is like watching the possible combinations of creation in a fluid genetic medium. And it is clear that somewhere at some level he *is* weeping despite himself: the code of 'full' and 'break' does its overflowing work, sobbed through the syntax. This is therefore one measure of how in the Shakespearean process words are not in control of all the thoughts and feelings they name or pass through: weeping, once summoned, breaks through the sentence which, like another part of the brain, seeks to wrest the tears to a willed conclusion. But the effect of the conflict only produces 'mad' instead of 'weep'. I have heard most actors say to the Fool, as Lear turns from his daughters, 'O fool, I shall go MAD'; but I once heard one actor stress it: 'O fool, I SHALL go mad', that thing Lear has been referring to and fearing repeatedly before now, which now feels inevitable. Both emphases are possible within the offered metrics, but not both together: what Shakespeare creates is the life-form that allows for minute but significant change and variation within it. Something is happening here, choices made at some deep level which exists *before* knowing, but out of which knowing itself comes.

But when we work at this level in Shakespeare, outside a teaching room or rehearsal studio, it can seem as if, in William James's words, we are catching snow-flakes and losing them even in the effort. A so-called 'close reading' of Shakespeare can take so long – can it not – for what is so little and so quick, and thus make static in print what is dynamic in time and practice. Actors are lucky, they can produce a sort of physical thinking on the spot: the performer of Macbeth in the very utterance of 'Curses, not loud but deep' can find the very difference of dimension between 'LOUD' and '*deep*' immediately within his own voice and know the meaning as by physiological pathways.[9] Later, perhaps, the actors cannot really say all they have done, nor feel the need to do so. But for those who are not actors, who want to make the experience last longer without becoming lesser, there is a problem about how to have some better grasp of this Shakespeare-thinking without thereby destroying it into a slow conceptualized aftermath.

This is where I want to begin to talk of what I shall call 'scanning', in what will turn out to be two senses of the word. Suppose for a moment we continue to work with the line/sentence code. Here, most famously, is Lear struggling back into mind, 'piecing it out', before Cordelia:

Methinks I should know you, and know this man;
Yet I am doubtful, for I am mainly ignorant
What place this is; and all the skill I have

> Remembers not these garments; nor I know not
> Where I did lodge last night.
>
>

The Tragedy of King Lear (Folio), 4.6.57–61

Three times here the lines break, in the face of all that this mind feels it '*should* know' and doesn't: 'mainly ignorant | What place this is'; 'all the skill I have | Remembers not these'; 'know not | Where I did lodge'. On one line there is the stumbling return of mind; on the other, equally, its own consciousness of all it cannot say or recognize; and together they are like the act of slowly coming back into mental focus amid 'the motes and shadows' of primal realization. It is so hard to form a sentence now. A positive sentence would be easy but, equally, unnecessary – 'I remember these garments; I know where I lodged last night.' But the sheer shock and shame of realizing how basic are these questions takes away the strength even to ask them direct: What place is this? Where did I lodge last night? Again the play says to Lear, 'Can'st make no use of nothing?' For this is the hardest thing, when all the intelligence that has gone into the evolution of a human gift or achievement, such as sentence-making, seems contradicted by the content of the sentences themselves. That is to say, Lear's sentence now has to admit: I understand that I do not understand at all. And that is a mental paradox symptomatic of a play where the force of life itself, even in its human capabilities, is what kills.

These line-endings are Shakespeare's implicit voice-directions to actors, but more than that. They are a form of slow-motion *eye*-map for actors' *voices* that offers deep insight into the workings of the human brain. For usually in our mental continuum we can only catch transitions when we happen to be arrested in our thinking, when we hesitate, for instance, in a sentence with a 'because' and the defeated forward movement of the mind is momentarily made the centre of attention. Without such total breakdown, Lear's line-endings here momentarily unveil 'thoughts in their dumb cradles' (*Troilus and Cressida*, 3.3.193).

But the speech does not stop at 'nor I know not | Where I did lodge last night', but like so much in *King Lear* goes on and on into the painful:

> Do not laugh at me
> For, as I am a man, I think this lady
> To be my child Cordelia.

4.6.61–4

Suppose we now imagine wiring the lines up to the sort of thought-experiment Hardy was carrying out in 'The Pedigree'. Imagine the old man's head now made transparent and that he is holding up a mirror to look inside it:

He pictured a metropolis, at once futuristic and ancient. Seen this way, his brain became a labyrinthine structure with vaults and chambers, floors and screens, columns, pathways, bridges, canals and aqueducts, with streams of information flowing in every direction. *Am I in there or out here?* he wondered.

'Am I out here or in there?'

First the thought, then the words. Thought. Speech. Thought. Speech. Alternating between the two, eyes fixed on the image in the mirror, he noticed a pattern, an ebbing and flowing of activity on the outer surface of the left frontal lobe. As he spoke, the soft mauve luminescence seemed to harden momentarily into a brighter glaze that dissolved as the utterance stopped … And where do thoughts and feelings come from? *Not me*, he thought because he saw that every fluctuation in the flow of experience, every intention and action, was anticipated by distinct tremors of activity across the brain's surface. It was not a case of thinking or doing something and watching the brain follow step or dance in synchrony. His brain was ahead of him. Ideas were bubbling up in the neuronal cauldron a good half-second before they appeared in consciousness.[10]

Perhaps it would be just as apt to have Hamlet wired up thus, with all those self-conscious efforts of his to get a hold on his own mental processes. For Claudius speaks of 'This something settled matter in his heart, | Whereon his brains still beating put him thus | From fashion of himself' (*Hamlet*, 3.1.176–8). Or Richard II imagining that in 'the hollow crown' about his temple, Death lurks and thinks and truly rules (*Richard II*, 3.2.156–66). Or Enobarbus's x-ray exposure of Antony: 'A diminution in our captain's brain | Restores his heart' (*Antony and Cleopatra*, 3.13.200–1).

But it is Lear here who does not know where he is and who is having to examine his own brain. And what makes 'I *think* this lady' light up on the brain-map of the page is a sort of backward synaptic connection with that earlier 'Methinks I *should know* you, and know this man' [my italics]. What is more, 'this lady' is like those other earlier deictic pointers – 'this man', 'what place this is', 'these garments' and (just before that) 'I will not swear *these* are *my* hands'. And yet, 'as I am a *man*', '*this lady*' manages to find the channel into '*my child*' [my italics] – across a gap every bit as perilous as, earlier, in:

> and to deal plainly /
> I fear I am not in my perfect mind

4.6.55–6

'*I* fear *I*' '*I am not* in *my* mind' [my italics]: these are shocking minute paradoxes caught in the midst of formulation. This is why I have Lear here wired up to the imaginary machine that actually is Shakespeare's verse of neural pathways: in Lear the ageing brain behind the mind is felt by the mind itself in its pauses. This is a language of stumbling connections, a braille by which a Gloucester would 'see it feelingly' (4.5.145), across and between the different senses in the 'labyrinthine structure'. This is thinking feeling its way through the channels of the brain:

Different ideas have their different 'feels', their immediate qualitative aspect, just as much as anything else. One who is thinking his way through a complicated problem finds direction in his way by means of this property of ideas. Their qualities stop him when he enters the wrong path and send him ahead when he hits the right one. They are signs of an intellectual 'Stop and go'. If a thinker had to work out the meaning of such ideas discursively, he would be lost in a labyrinth that had no end and no centre.[11]

Thus the 'feel' lodged in the temporary 'stop' between 'to deal plainly' and 'I fear I am not in my perfect mind' and, again, between 'I think this lady' and 'To be my child, Cordelia' is precisely what gets articulated en route to those utterances in those painful words 'Do not laugh at me'. But where, out of the blue, on Lear's awakening, did this thought of being laughed at suddenly come from? The whole speech began, of course, 'Pray do not mock me. | I am a very foolish fond old man …' But the real answer is that the fear of mockery suddenly comes from all those earlier memories of being humiliated in the play. Threatening to make cruel Laughter mentally present on stage, in the ghostly persons of those other two daughters, those past humiliations have now visibly become a confirmed pathway in Lear's brain and caught in a time-lag which Cordelia has to witness in tears.

I am saying that in such ways Shakespeare's lines are Renaissance brain scanners, where scanning is to do both with poetic rhythm and with neurological patterning. From eye to voice or ear to eye, from text to performance, in the interplay of line and sentence or metre and rhythm, between brain and mind: these are the great Shakespearean shifts of mentality, to and fro.

This is what is so remarkable about Shakespeare – that, unlike the man in Broks' story held between thought and speech, Shakespeare is so *un*afraid of the brain beneath the mind, sending its messages in advance of realization. 'Every intention and action, was *anticipated* by distinct tremors of activity across the brain's surface. His brain was ahead of him. Ideas were bubbling up in the neuronal cauldron a good half-second before they appeared in consciousness.' In Lear, of course, at the moment of his terrible reawakening, the brain–mind process is profoundly slowed. But what it means in Shakespeare, in general, is that thoughts create and come out of a fundamental *excitement*, as the brain lights up and fires. That physical firing of realization means, moreover, that there is some deeply-rooted, pre-verbal *excess* of significance which comes not only before but also over and above any particular linguistic attempt at formulating it. That excess beneath is what Bergson called the 'fringe' around:

> The feeling we have of our evolution . . . is there, forming around the intellectual concept properly so-called an indistinct fringe that fades off into darkness . . .
>
> Indeed, if the fringe exists, however delicate and indistinct, it should have more importance for philosophy than the bright nucleus it surrounds. For it is its presence that enables us to affirm that the nucleus is a nucleus, that pure intellect is a contraction, by condensation of a more extensive power.[12]

It is Shakespeare's dramatically poetic language that does most to summon that fringe, that resonance of all which lies around and beneath it. Hence the sudden flashes of emotion it gives off. For emotion is both the sign of that unsaid and unsayable excess and the neural messenger that brings the feel of it into consciousness.

Indeed, in this condensing style, Shakespeare writes so fast, with so physical a mentality, as to blur mind into brain, feeling the electric flash of thought between one phrase and another even *before* the second one is quite created. 'Do not laugh at me' has been there with him so long before it is finally uttered. It is like the voice heard within Macbeth: 'Methought I heard a voice cry, "Sleep no more"' (*Macbeth*, 2.2.38). That quick-forging, silent inner voice of suggestion that Shakespeare picked up from within himself is the great Shakespearean discovery, the tacit physical messenger in the act of accelerated poetic thinking.[13] It is what he hears or senses electrically in the swift interstices of formulation. The human brain – registered as momentarily prior to its mental formulations – is here at its demonstrably most creative: for in Shakespeare you can see not only the results of his discoveries but also the *live* near-physiological process of his making them.

3 A Shakespearean Grammar

In 1864, at the age of only 26, Edwin A. Abbott became head-master of the City of London School, where he served until 1889, becoming one of the most admired teachers of his age. Immediately upon his appointment – though he had just come from being a fel-low in Classics at St John's College, Cambridge – he went beyond the traditional school curriculum in Latin and Greek, introducing the study of English Literature, as well as the sciences. From an arti-cle on 'The Teaching of English' which he published in *Macmillan's Magazine* in 1868, and from the introduction and the 'notes and questions' section in his *Shakespearian Grammar* of 1869, it is pos-sible to reconstruct something of what a pioneering lesson in think-ing about Shakespeare would have been like over 150 years ago.

Set out in solid sections simply labelled 'Adjectives', 'Prepositions' and so on, and with numbered paragraphs for each sub-section of examples, A *Shakespearian Grammar* looks like what it is only in part – an exhaustively useful book of reference for all the difficulties of Shakespeare's syntax and prosody. But beneath that, in its pas-sionate accumulation, it is also a way of learning a whole language. The difficulties, said Abbott, were not to do with individual words, which could always be looked up in a glossary; they were to do with a whole idiom. So Abbott begins by telling students about the dif-ference between Elizabethan and modern English. He says of the dramatic nature of Elizabethan grammar in general: 'It was com-mon to place words in the order in which they came uppermost in the mind, without much regard to syntax, and the result was a forcible and perfectly unambiguous but ungrammatical sentence.' He gives an example of this Elizabethan commitment to succinct compression from *The Rape of Lucrece* – on time as the tempting provider of opportunity, setting the wolf far too close to the lamb:

> O hear me then, injurious shifting time;
> *Be guilty of my death, since of my crime –*
>
> [my italics]

Since [you are guilty] of my crime. It is just such ellipses, such accelerated and energizing compactions that most interest Abbott, ignoring as they do the serially unfolding subject-verb-object order of Victorian English. 'One great cause of the difference between Elizabethan and Victorian English is that the latter has introduced or developed what may be called the *division of labour*.' Where, for instance, an Elizabethan might tersely say, 'Make peace *of* enmity' (*Richard III*, 2.1.51), Abbott's Victorian speaker would say more methodically, 'Make peace *instead of* enmity' [my italics] – thus not making one word almost immediately out of another, but rather spelling and spreading the meaning out, 'diminishing the task assigned to overburdened words', so as to divide and share the labour of expression. It is as though such Victorian prose exists to fill in, or spell out, the meaningful gaps for inference left by the compression of the Elizabethan message: at its best, it is not tame paraphrase so much as the receiving partner in meaning, the mental legatee that the poetry sought. Indeed, from Newman's *Essay on the Development of Christian Doctrine* to Darwin's *The Origin of Species*, that is what the later nineteenth century often characteristically thought itself to be: the conscious receiver of the explicit working-out of implicit codes, as they realized themselves in the long course of history.

Abbott thus warned his students that 'The Elizabethan authors objected to scarcely any ellipsis, provided the deficiency could be easily supplied from the context.' The Elizabethans were used to involving an audience or a readership in filling in the rest. But their implicit priority is that Mind comes before formal Syntax – though arguably this happens not quite 'without much regard to syntax' as Abbott puts it, but rather through the adaptation of grammar, in the second place, to the spaces that the excited mind, at the first, leaves and finds for it. As Hazlitt had said, Shakespeare's words 'seem to know their places' ('On Shakspeare and Milton', *Lectures on the English Poets*, 1818). They seem summoned by a momentary pre-vision of the gaps, spaces and contours of situation, which they turn into realized shapes and syntax.

At any rate, Abbott set his class of 15-year-olds to study Shakespeare's *Richard II*. They were to consider the speech of the Duchess of Gloucester to John of Gaunt, where she complains of his lack of response to the loss of her husband, his brother: 'Call it not patience, Gaunt, it is despair' (1.2.29). The teacher asked: How is it decided which is the *right* word to 'call it' by? Then he wrote out two further lines:

> That which in mean men we entitle patience
> Is pale cold cowardice in noble breasts.
>
> 33–4

Across what are, characteristically, two different *lines* of thought in Shakespeare, that which is called the virtue of 'patience' for 'mean men' may become the vice of 'cowardice' relative to 'noble' ones. The inferred context makes the difference. The teacher then recalled one other line from Mowbray in the play's opening scene: 'Yet can I not of such tame patience boast | As to be hushed ...' (1.1.52–3). 'What is the difference', Abbott asks finally, 'between "patience" and "tameness", "patience" and "despair", "tameness" and "cowardice"?'

Though demanding of accuracy of attention, this wasn't a mere pedantic formalism. Abbott insisted that by asking his precise questions he was teaching not only 'the knowledge of words' but through them also 'the knowledge of thoughts and the power of thinking'. The process of what Coleridge called 'desynonymising' was what E. A. Abbott was carrying out in his classroom. When words, introduced into the language, find 'the broader room which they had been intended to fill already occupied', says Abbott, they 'were forced to take narrower meanings'. This is what happens in the gradual process of the evolution of a language, as the words find room for their place or niche in the system of thought.

But Richard II himself calls it a setting of 'the word itself | Against the word' (*Richard II*, 5.5.13–14, Quarto) – because in Shakespeare, as at the very beginning of things, there is no gradual evolution but an *accelerated* struggle for verbal existence in the dramatic working out of meaning. With both borrowings from the classics and native neologisms, the period from 1570 to 1630 provided the fastest growing vocabulary in the history of English, pushing the very limits of grammar. However familiar, there is no more important fact in the story of Shakespeare's emergence. Shakespeare is the highest expression of that historical phenomenon.

Thus, for example, in *Coriolanus* there gathers around the impact of the protagonist, in his so-called 'pride', a whole competing spectrum of words and meanings offered – stretching all the way from arrogant 'obstinacy' at one extreme to heroic 'constancy' at another. If what in *Richard II* is 'patience' in one line but 'cowardice' in another, then Coriolanus intuitively understands what the Shakespearean interrelation of words to lines stands for, when he himself says of the Romans:

> I had rather be *their servant* in *my* way
> Than *rule* with them in *theirs*.
>
> 2.1.200–1 [my italics]

His way of finding a *place* of meaning for himself in this world is to make proud service not an oxymoron but a bearable alternative to the intolerable paradox of weak leadership.

This was the same E. A. Abbott who in 1884, while still a headmaster, was to write *Flatland: a Romance of Many Dimensions*, in which he satirically imagines a creature who, living inside a two-dimensional plane, is roused to ascend to a three-dimensional world called Spaceland. The flat creature gets there only by first going down to the lower realm of Lineland and then Pointland – closed worlds that can no more imagine a higher dimension, he realizes, than he himself could within the bounds of Flatland:

> Behold yon miserable creature. That Point is a Being like ourselves, but confined to the non-dimensional Gulf. He is himself his own World, his own Universe; of any other than himself he can form no conception; he knows not Length, nor Breadth, nor Height, for he has had no experience of them; he has no cognizance even of the number Two; nor has he a thought of Plurality; for he is himself his One and All, being really Nothing. Yet mark his perfect self-contentment, and hence learn this lesson, that to be self-contented is to be vile and ignorant, and that to aspire is better than to be blindly and impotently happy.[1]

Beyond the world of Pointland, where there is no communication, creatures in the acoustic universe of Lineland communicate across space by sound-vibrations, and reproduce by a form of music. By such acts of (as it were) reverse imagination, in imagining *less* than he knows now, Abbott's protagonist from Flatland is equivalently impelled, by analogy, in some sense to try to 'see' *more* than his own two dimensions tell him. For this is a mind now straining blindly to think outside its own framework or configuration. The book becomes a work of creative geometry. In it, it is easy for creatures in every dimension to look down on the level below them and see the limitations; what is harder is to imagine that their own dimension is, likewise, not the ultimate one. That difficult imagination he calls Thoughtland, and he tries to hold on to his intimation of an extra dimension by repeating the mantra 'Upwards, and yet not Northwards' – since in his world's terms, northwards would only take him along existing lines, not above them. Where he cannot truly see, except through the mind's eye, it is words which are the necessary holdfast to the possibility of an invisible reality: 'Upwards, and yet not Northwards … I determined steadfastly to retain these words as the clue' (p. 107). Yet all the time, despite this blind language, he feels his vision of something-more 'in some strange way slipping away from me, like the image of a half-grasped, tantalizing dream' (p. 112). Partly to hold on to his own lesson, he tries unavailingly to teach it to others in his world, despite the state laws against such thinking: 'with the view of evading the Law, if possible, I spoke not of a physical Dimension, but of a Thoughtland whence, in theory, a Figure could look down upon Flatland and see simultaneously the in-side of all things' (p. 114). To be inside a framework and yet at the same time to be able somehow to think outside or above it, is the challenge.

There is an implicit connection between *Flatland* and *A Shakespearian Grammar*, published 15 years earlier, which has never been fully acknowledged but which shows Abbott's deeper intentions as going beyond the writing of his austere student primer. The epigraph for the journey into Other Worlds in *Flatland* is an adaptation of Miranda's words near the end of *The Tempest*: 'O brave new worlds, that have such people in them!', just as the epigraph for the opening part is taken from *Romeo and Juliet*: 'Be patient, for the world is broad and wide'. For what the audience 'see' in Shakespeare, from outside the stage, is itself a sort of Thoughtland, working imaginatively in varying geometric dimensions and through different human senses. By means of his very syntax Shakespeare was for Abbott the great explorer of all the overlapping dimensions of meaning, massed together at speed. For the deepest language of thinking in Shakespeare is not to do with nouns and names, or with categories and explanations, but with the spaces and journeys between them. It is to do with the sort of resonant mental space that Abbott was investigating *between* the words 'patience', 'despair' and 'tameness', as they emerge from the same broad pool or continuum of human character. These are not just separate, static names: what Abbott is investigating is how, across their boundaries, these words call each other forth, in thought, choice and competition, as in the very formation of the language-field itself.

The mental spaces between these words exist just as surely on the stage, in their own dimension, as do the physical spaces between the characters. Thus it is characteristic of Abbott to take a quick shape-shifting line from Macbeth, on Macbeth's seeing Banquo's blood on the first Murderer's face – ''Tis better thee without than he within' (3.4.13) – and then in the Notes and Questions for further exercises, at the end of his *Shakespearian Grammar*, to ask in his school-masterly voice: 'Meaning? Comment on the syntax.' But this is not just an exercise for schoolboys. One scene is almost physically turned into another when the blood that was within Banquo's veins in 3.3 is now so visibly upon the murderer's face in 3.4. ''Tis better thee without than he within' then also means 'I'd rather come up against a hideous blood-stained monster like you – in the clear and limited physical world – than be penetrated and invaded even unto my heart of hearts by Banquo.'

For all the careful pedagogic cataloguing of types and variations in his Victorian *Grammar*, Abbott understood the Elizabethan dynamic. On the very first page of his introduction he quotes what he takes to be a characteristic Elizabethan move even in the occasional, witty verses of Thomas Heywood who:

> after dividing human dinners into three classes thus –
> > Some with small fare they be not pleased,
> > Some with much fare they be diseased,
> > Some with mean fare be scant appeased

> adds with true Elizabethan freedom –
> > But of all *somes* none is displeased
> > > To be welcome.

Suddenly in the fourth line that word 'some' is seized, used to pull the other three indefinite pronouns into itself, and then wittily put back into line, with 'all' on one side and 'none' on the other, like a noun transformed. In that extraordinary mixture of thrift, richness and mobility to be found in Elizabethan English, 'almost any part of speech', concludes Abbott, 'can be used as any other part of speech'. This lifting, turning and new-weighting of the word – technically now known as '(word-class) conversion' or 'functional shift', from one part of speech to another without change in itself – is, I want to say, a source of fresh energy that charges and changes the space all around it, raising the meaning to a new level, letting it leap into a different dimension. Functional shift is what we might now think of as a classic Darwinian example of economy: a single form serving multiple functions; or it is what an Elizabethan might call infinite riches in a little room. I want now to create a context in which to show functional shift as a central clue to Shakespearean thinking.

Beyond Flatland: Of Lines and Levels

In his little book *Evoking Shakespeare*, the theatre-director Peter Brook has a complicated thing to say about how Shakespeare goes beyond one-directional storytelling and the mere surface of action:

> At each second he was conscious not only of the action itself but also of the relationships on an infinite number of levels that were connected to that action. So he was forced to develop for himself a very extraordinary and complex instrument which we call 'poetry', by which within one single line he could give both the narrative meaning and at the same time find the appropriate words that contain the resonances that bring together all the different levels of association that he was carrying within him.[2]

Once again I need to use Shakespeare in slow motion to think about this relationship between 'levels' and 'lines'. And what makes it slow-motion in the following is the deliberate absence of the sort of dynamic that goes into functional shift. It is Edmund's bitter opening speech in *King Lear*, the Folio version, on being the bastard son of Gloucester:

> Well then,
> Legitimate Edgar, I must have your land.
> Our father's love is to the bastard Edmond
> As to th'legitimate. Fine word, 'legitimate'.
> Well, my legitimate, if this letter speed
> And my intention thrive, Edmond the base
> Shall to th'legitimate. I grow, I prosper.

The Tragedy of King Lear, 1.2.15–21

I don't mind if modern editors sometimes emend that last line to 'Shall top th'legitimate', with 'top' playing off against 'base': it is probably half-there anyway. What I do somewhat mind is those inverted commas that are put around 'legitimate', as earlier in the speech indignantly around 'bastard' and 'base': 'Why "bastard"? Wherefore "base"?', 'Why brand they us | With "base", with "baseness, bastardy – base, base"–' (1.2.6, 9–10). It is not so punctuated in the Folio, which goes more with the use of the colon and the capital letter: 'Our Fathers love, is to the Bastard Edmond | As to th'legitimate: fine word: Legitimate.' The point is that, in his relentless narrative focus on the idea of 'legitimacy', the change of level should be heard but little seen. What is happening is that certain words – bastard, base, legitimate – are being taken out of the lines, are being *lifted* out of their initial grammatical and social context, and then are reinstated back in, with a concomitant shift in tone and direction. The dimension is changed till Edmund can speak in lines that are now a kind of vertical summit to what preceded them: from base to top, 'I grow'. The rule is: the less the overt punctuation, the more the inner cerebration – where by 'punctuation' I mean any visual or explicit mark spelling out a change in modality. The less of that, the more we have to work out the levels from inside the lines. Punctuation is really best represented in terms of pause, pace, shift, contour. What Shakespeare wants is a syntax as close as possible to an ever-flowing, shifting stream, in which the changes and minute stops-and-goes are still caught within the continual ongoingness. That is what William James, for example, loves about thinking-in-process: it unstiffens all our theories, thereby releasing unprogrammed responses from the tyranny of thinking in abstraction and in advance.

Even when Shakespeare does use overt repetition, it is rarely lame or tautological, never truly on just the same line of thought. I think again here of something I have tried to think out before – the opening of Sonnet 128: 'How oft when thou, my music, music play'st …'. The poet hears his beloved playing something as beautiful to the *ear* as she herself is, simultaneously, to the *eye*. It would not be anything like so good if it were spelled out as a main clause along the line, slowly left to right, one thing after another: You play music and you are my music too. The implosive effect is partly to do with that hidden inner contrapuntal or backwards movement 'when thou, my music, music play'st' – making 'music, music' cry out in its own voice from the magnetic middle of the line, like sudden love. But what is also so breathtaking is the anticipatory leap of thought, the tacit metaphor 'my music' getting in fractionally *before* the literal playing of music from which it must have derived. It is like Orsino's talk of the music of a sweet wind 'stealing and giving' odour from a bed of violets at the beginning of *Twelfth Night*: the word is lifted *out* of the line onto a different and almost transcendental level, but then silently given back to remain immanent *within* it again. Where 'a' is one word-phrase and 'c' is another, Shakespeare will often get from 'a' to 'c' (or 'd' or …) by omitting 'b', the inner means by which he got there. But the link 'b' is usually some fast-suppressed version of modified repetition or alternative variation which invisibly ratchets up the level whilst continuing along the time-passing line.

So, as with 'music', the act of repetition in Edmund's speech means that you have time to *see*, within his vengeful wit, the lifting of the thought from out of the word and the putting it back down again with different spin in a new context. 'Well, my legitimate …' But in functional shift, I now want to say, the repetition is precisely what is omitted: Shakespeare's Coriolanus isn't going to say 'he treated me like a god – I might almost say he godded me even'. He says: 'This last old man … Lov'd me above the measure of a father | Nay, *godded* me indeed' (*Coriolanus*, 5.3.8–11) [my italics]. The process is swallowed up within itself: there is a leap, the verb coming out of the noun even *before* the noun is sounded. Functional shift is, as Abbott helps us realize, a super-fast version of metaphor as compressed simile. When Antony speaks of the supporters that had previously '*spaniell'd* me at heels', he means the men who followed him at his heels '*like spaniels*' (*Antony and Cleopatra*, 4.13.20–1). This, then, so speeded up and compressed, is the Shakespeare thing itself: functional shift.

George Puttenham called it '*enallage* or the figure of exchange' when the Greeks and Latins 'changed not the very word, but kept the word and changed the shape of him only' (*The Arte of English Poesie*, 1589, 3, 15). The powerful and fast economy thus involved, when one part of speech becomes another with different *function* but without change of *form*, resulted from the loss of inflectional endings in the early Middle Ages. Without the need for endings that distinguished a verb, say, by the suffix 'en', Shakespeare was able to draw freedom and power from the very imprecisions of English grammar, as Abbott himself was one of the first to note in detail. 'In the general destruction of inflections which prevailed during the Elizabethan period, *en* was particularly discarded,' he writes in paragraph 290 of *A Shakespearian Grammar* – though its work in the conversion of noun or adjective into verb can still be seen with 'heart' becoming 'hearten', 'light' 'lighten', 'glad' 'gladden'. 'But though the infinitive inflection was generally dropped.' Abbott goes on, 'the converting power was retained, undiminished by the absence of the condition. Hence it may be said that any noun or adjective could be converted into a verb by the Elizabethan authors.' As he puts it in the introduction, 'You can "happy" your friend, "malice" or "foot" your enemy, or "fall" axe on his neck.'

I want to argue that this is not just a stylistic or historical detail: functional shift is characteristic of Shakespeare thinking. It is a micro-version of all manner of larger boundary-shifts in the work in general – as, for example, Lear in the storm, and the storm also in Lear; or, Iago functioning as both himself and a part of Othello.

In paragraph 290 Abbott easily lists over 50 key examples of functional shift in Shakespeare, adding another 20 in paragraph 451. In the classroom he might write out the example, italicize the shift word, and then ask his pupils to say what part of speech it constituted. By this means, as they hesitated, he could show the students how what was originally an *adjective* was in passage to becoming a *verb* (and I shall italicize words in the following examples for emphasis) – as when Polixenes says that his young son 'cures in me | Thoughts that would *thick* my blood (*The Winter's Tale*, 1.2.170–1); or Antony reassures Cleopatra that 'that which most with you should *safe* my going | Is Fulvia's death' (*Antony and Cleopatra*, 1.3.55–6); or Henry V cries to any brave common man at Agincourt that 'be he ne'er so vile | This day shall *gentle* his condition' (*Henry V*, 4.3.62–3). He could also show them how *pronouns* are made into *nouns* – 'you are the cruellest *she* alive' (*Twelfth Night*, 1.5.230), or how *nouns* turn *adjectives* – the last minute being 'A time methinks too short | To make a *world-without-end* bargain in' (*Love's Labours Lost*, 5.2.780–1). Equally, *verbs* could become *nouns* – 'There's something in his soul | O'er which his melancholy sits on brood | And I do doubt *the hatch and the disclose* | Will be some danger' (*Hamlet*, 3.1.167–70). Or an *adverb* might convert into a *verb* – in *The Rape of Lucrece*, 'O, how are they wrapped in with infamies | That from their own deeds *askance* their eyes!' (636–7); or again in the words of France, taking Cordelia in marriage, though her father banishes her: 'Thou losest *here*, a better *where* to find' (*King Lear*, 1.1.261). Then also, an *adverb* might find itself a *noun*: as in Prospero's 'What seest thou else | In the dark *backward* and abyss of time?' (*The Tempest*, 1.2.49–50). Shakespeare even laughs at his own process when in *Twelfth Night* Sir Toby urges Andrew Aguecheek to 'accost' Maria: 'Accost, Sir Andrew, Accost … My niece's chambermaid', but the simple passive knight only addresses her instead: 'Good Mistress Mary Accost, I desire better acquaintance' (1.3.46–50). The *verb* becomes *noun*.

But, above all, the shift-type most expressive of all that conversion meant was that from *noun* to *verb*. For that is what conversion is most about, shifting from static names to dynamic processes – and not by bringing in verbs in place of nouns but by making nouns turn into them. For as I said in Chapter 1, Shakespeare's whole language at its inception is quintessentially more like the work of a verb than a noun. As Abbott notes in paragraph 518, the whole process is related to the silent compression of simile into metaphor, as in 'the ship *ploughs* the sea', or 'no more shall trenching war *channel* her fields (*1 Henry IV*, 1.1.7). The words are manhandled into the very 'shape' of active thinking by a swift transforming act of almost physical mentality. Thus, the examples of verbs made out of nouns are most plentiful and most powerful:

- 'Nature prompts them | in simple and low things to *prince* it' (*Cymbeline*, 3.3.84–5);
- 'How light and portable my pain seems now, | When that which makes me bend makes the king bow. | He *childed* as I *fathered*' (*King Lear*, Quarto, 3.6.101–3);
- 'To *lip* a wanton in a secure couch | And to suppose her chaste!' (*Othello*, 4.1.70–1);
- 'Would'st thou be *windowed* in great Rome?' (*Antony and Cleopatra*, 4.15.72);
- 'My becomings kill me when they do not | *Eye* well to you' (*Antony and Cleopatra*, 1.3.97–8);
- 'Fall down, and *knee* | The way into his mercy' (*Coriolanus*, 5.1.5–6).

Gods in men, princes in peasants; lips and eyes and knees felt in thought – these are some of the effects of this sheer *making* of a world to dwell in, to the utmost of one's powers. Ezra Pound offered an example in English of the transference of force that he found in the concision of Chinese notation: 'dog *attending* man = dogs him'. So Antony's followers 'spaniell'd him' at the heels. Pound's mentor in this, the orientalist Ernest Fenollosa concluded:

> A true noun, an isolated thing, does not exist in nature. Things are only the terminal points, or rather the meeting points, of actions, cross-sections cut through actions, snapshots … The eye sees noun and verb as one: things in motion, motion in things.[3]

One path or one speech crosses another; one word meets a second; a minute pause in the midst of things momentarily affects whatever is on either side of itself: in all these meeting-points in the process, the happening happens before we can register it, at some microscopic transition-point we can never reach. This is the power and energy of life that flows – things in motion, motion in things – as when Florizel praises Perdita's dancing like 'a wave o' th' sea, that you ever do | Nothing but that, move *still, still* so' [my italics] (*The Winter's Tale*, 4.4.141–2).

Sometimes you can witness those junction-points. The very processes of functional shift are epitomized within another characteristic form of language-thinking in Shakespeare, called *hendiadys* – meaning, literally, the figure of 'one through two'. Two substantives are joined by an 'and' to force an implied mental connection, usually far less obvious than its seeming innocence implies: 'In Shakespeare's practice, the second [noun] may unfold the first ("*ponderous and marble*") or the first the second ("*from cheer and from your former state*"); or one may logically modify the other ("*law and heraldry*" for "heraldic law"); or, as is most usual, the parallel structure may mask some more complex and less easily describable dependent relation ("sweet, not lasting | The *perfume and suppliance of a minute*").'[4] Thus there is the split-linking of 'seeds | *And* weak beginnings' or 'hatch *and* brood' (*2 Henry IV*, 3.1.79–81). Yet at other times the 'and' disappears. Macbeth brings together just two words to make the compound, 'mouth-honour' (5.3.27); as does Ariel in the contrasting coinage of the necessity for 'heart-sorrow' (*The Tempest*, 3.3.81).

All this, I am saying, is language in the midst and the mix of the life it depicts. It knows the very processes of transference and transmutation, as it works in and out of different modes. At the very heart of Shakespeare's creativity, the language of functional shift makes new life out of basic materials which it does not need to change, only to adapt and blend and charge. The reach at one word pulls out another; the super-charged space between them has further thoughts and possibilities hidden in the dark behind it. The physical equivalent or 'type' of such sentences in the world of nature, says Fenollosa, is a flash of lightning. So it is in the theatre as Vives describes it in *Fabula de Homine* (1518): the gods look down on the play of life on earth and suddenly find themselves so powerfully represented on the stage before them that they do not know quite where they are.

But above all, what is characteristic of Shakespeare is a further compression of these processes: the quasi-synaptic connection made between one thought-firing word and another is silent, invisible, subterranean, without obvious repetition or simile, without even the summoning 'and' or the traceable shift. Exeter, for example, speaks of how he tried not to weep in the face of the death of his fellow-nobles at Agincourt:

> But I had not so much of man in me,
> And all my mother came into mine eyes
> And gave me up to tears.
>
> *Henry V*, 4.6.30–2

'So much of man' there lays hold of that word 'man', trying to bring its abbreviated essence within this particular specimen. In a lesser thinker, 'man' in that line would simply take the established pathway to 'woman' in the next ('woman me unto't' in *All's Well That Ends Well*, 3.2.51 would nicely express how unmanned Exeter felt in crying like a woman). But Shakespeare has already assumed the obvious and leap-frogged over it by making the unspoken 'woman' 'mother' – partly because it is to do with the death of brother-nobles; partly because he feels not just like a woman but like a grown-up and now uncomforted child; and partly because as with 'hysterico passio' in Lear's 'O how this mother swells up toward my heart', hysteria is a disease of the womb (*The Tragedy of King Lear*, 2.2.231–2).[5] 'Man-woman' would go along the lines pretty much at stand-still, already known in advance; but 'man-mother' shows Shakespeare's verbal thinking suddenly leaping, as Hazlitt said, into the future which it thereby makes for itself – leaving all that tacitly went into its formulation to explode upon the audience in its wake. Exeter does not just say, simply and separately: I felt like a woman and a mother, or I thought of my own mother, or I felt like my mother's child again. Rather, the words are grown as dense as the predicament in which he finds himself – which is all that Shakespeare ever seeks, to surround someone with the raw excess material for the possible meaning of his life. This is what I think Peter Brook means by 'words that contain the resonances that bring together all the different levels of association' – poetry is the densest, quickest medium:

> And all my mother came into mine eyes
> And gave me up to tears.

Even more than the phrase '*so much* of man', '*all* my mother' here is the sign of a an invisible verbal power seizing the word 'mother', and shifting it from a real person to a verbal thought. And that 'mother' should suddenly come into my '*eyes*' (not mind) is again characteristic of how a Shakespearian *line* so often seems almost physically to shake us by its power to fuse elements brought together from different *levels*, varying registers or contexts. It is like

Leontes wishing that the '*magic*' at the end of *The Winter's Tale* should be an art 'lawful as eating' (5.3.111). But like 'music' in Sonnet 128, 'mother' is transportable into metaphor here by the sheer ability of the *thing or person* to be a *word*. That capacity briefly releases Shakespeare's brain from the *feeling* of the thing, for this purpose: that the word can momentarily hold the *thought* of that feeling for him instead, and he can then immediately transfer its energy into making the next move in search of the play's verbal future.

Here, for example, is a man lying asleep on the ground, no better than the earth he lies upon: 'If he were that which now he's like – that's dead' (*The Tempest*, 2.1.287). 'That' twice over is likewise a wonderful swift syntactic interchange of energies from thought into word, from word back into further thought. And thus the shift from literal to metaphorical and back becomes so blurred in the speech from *Henry V* that when Exeter finally says 'and gave *me* up to *tears*' [my italics], he really, physically means it – the solid 'I' so dissolved that I am all tears now.

Through the minute gap between thought and word, word and further thought, Shakespeare can 'steal and give' meaning, catching suggestion even from his own utterances. It is like a swift internal version of what Ophelia's hearers do more mistakenly in the face of those mad sayings 'that carry but half sense':

> Her speech is nothing,
> Yet the unshapèd use of it doth move
> The hearers to collection. They aim at it,
> And botch the words up fit to their own thought
>
> *Hamlet*, 4.5.7–10

Shakespeare 'collects' and 'shapes' out of his own speech. As ever, he can twist and turn both ways, give meaning to words, and take meaning from them, always with that tiny space, that little leap, that minute time-lag to work in, between the words and the meanings. So when Ariel reports to Prospero that if he now saw his enemies so trapped, his emotions would soften and become tender, the space between words is further opened by dialogue:

PROSPERO: Dost thou think so, spirit?
ARIEL: Mine would, sir, were I human.

The Tempest, 5.1.19–20

In Hazlitt's terms, what Ariel *transmits* as *word* from the other side, as spirit, Prospero must *receive* and pick up on his side as *meaning* again: that outside word 'human' explodes within him, as what within himself he now is again.

ARIEL: *Mine would*, sir, were I *human.*
PROSPERO: And *mine shall*

The Tempest, 5.1.30–1 [my italics]

What is lifted out is returned back again, within. It is like that great moment in *Twelfth Night* when Viola says in her double language:

My father had a daughter lov'd a man
As it might be, perhaps, were I a woman,
I should your lordship.

DUKE: And what's her history?

A blank, my lord. She never told her love

Twelfth Night, 2.4.107–10

It isn't linearly 'my father had a daughter *who one day grew up to* love a man'. Even more vitally, it isn't 'as, were I a woman, I should *love* your lordship'. The omitted repetition of 'love', which here indeed she never told, quietly explodes there in the audience's mind even as 'human' does in Prospero's: 'It gives a very echo to the seat | Where love is throned' (2.4.20–1). The ellipses, the fast-tracked omissions are summed up in that powerful phrase 'a blank', into which the word 'love' goes: 'a blank' is the explicit name for that empty-seeming space of potential, so often present within the gaps and leaps between the words, from which are generated all the suggestive possibilities that may or may not finally come into being in Shakespeare.

And at 'A blank, my lord', the poetry momentarily stops (it's a colon in the Folio, not a full-stop) – and also still can't quite: 'She never told her love'. At other such moments, the poetry, like Ariel, suddenly drinks the air before it (*The Tempest*, 5.1.104), creating a momentary vacuum to fill, further on ahead. It does not simply move forward, it pulls what is immediately before back behind itself, in order rhythmically to lever itself on. In Clarence's nightmare of drowning:

> still the envious flood
> Stopped in my soul and would not let it forth
> To find the empty, vast, and wand'ring air,
> But smothered it within my panting bulk
> Who almost burst ...

> *Richard III*, 1.4.37–41

It is clearly not that the flood leisurely stopped in(side) my soul: the whole momentum up to that 'burst' is created by the fact that the flood 'stopped-in' (held in) my soul. That sudden pull-back into suffix of that little word 'in' is what pushes the meaning on forward amid the resistances to come.

Such are the ways in which the mind – immersed in the feel of its own language predicament and struggling to make itself out – is given something back from its own felt process, even as it goes along. Certain words, phrases, even structures and rhythms act as hidden gateways between levels in the dense network of relations. Different ideas, said John Dewey, have their different 'feels': someone thinking his way through a complicated problem, that could not be worked out discursively, finds direction by means of these signals of 'stop' or 'go'.

We need to learn Shakespearean grammar – and it is Edwin Abbott who is the first basic teacher. Something of what, more broadly, Shakespeare's grammar represented for Abbott is given in what the Latinate grammar of John Milton meant to Abbott's contemporary, the scientist John Tyndall:

> English grammar was the most important discipline of my boy-hood. The piercing through the involved and inverted sentences of *Paradise Lost*, the linking of the verb to its often distant nom-inative, of the relative to its transitive verb, of the preposition to the noun or pronoun which it governed, the study of variations in mood or tense, the transpositions often necessary to bring out the true grammatical structure of a sentence, all this was to my young mind a discipline of the highest value, and a source of unflagging delight.

This is about a language which is not linearly straightforward but demands a spatial imagination, a sense of layers and interrelation-ships in space, beyond the single plane of Flatland – for 'poetry works by cross-setting a considerable number of systems in simul-taneity (natural speech word order, metric units, line units, gram-matical units, cursive syntax – all play across each other)'.[6]

In this broad sense of grammar, I am arguing that Shakespeare's words are not simply inserted into a pre-formed grammar-box; that, equally, his protagonists are not just defined by a set name or con-cept; that minds will not stay within their bodies; and that, finally, his thoughts and his people are not merely contained within the bounds of a settled world. In the classical mathematical physics that Newton was to bring to Shakespeare's world, space and time were made external to the entities that make up the universe: they served as the fundamental receptacle or frame of reference. But in Shakespeare each happening dramatically or magically changes the shape of its world in a moment or, as latter-day process philosophers were to put it, each occasion creates space-time in and around itself, as part of its very occurrence. It is like the flash of lightning in *King Lear* felt by the old man as though it were a terrible thought from the world's brain electrifying his own head too. And all the more, of course, does Shakespeare's world change its sheer dimensions in a flash of 'thought-executing fires' when it is a world made of words (*The Tragedy of King Lear*, 3.2.4).

Some art historians have likened the Renaissance emphasis on sentence-making, with the end kept carefully in sight, to the equally space-orientating discovery, in painting, of fixed-point perspective, such that all the elements in a composition give the impression of continuous recession from a single viewing-point.[7] But actually, this is more like Dryden's perspectival requirement that in his rewritings of Shakespeare there should be a single point of sight in which all the lines finally terminate.[8] Shakespeare is closer to Renaissance tricks of double perspective. For the shape of a thing depends on the perspective – shift it ever so slightly and the 'object' changes. So, Edgar on Dover cliff has different perspectives in the same painting, with different vanishing points. In that sense Shakespeare is more like a cubist in action: taking multiple points of view almost simultaneously until it is not two or three people separately inserted into one solidly external situational container so much as two or three reciprocally overlapping situations within one complex blended happening. It is as though the occasion itself, like a living thing, knows nothing about the parts within itself being separate or, at least, thinking themselves to be so. It is we who habitually think in terms of subject and object: in the overlaps that go on in *Measure for Measure*, for example, we might still see it all separately – in terms of Isabella having *this* thought but Angelo having *that* one about her and *another* one about Claudio, all in Act 2, Scene 4; or again, in the subsequent scene, Claudio, the subject of their conversation, facing the death penalty all on his own. But Shakespeare's grammar, both literal and psychological, is radically different. Angelo himself knows this, when he has to work out how he can be 'tempted' by a woman even without her knowing it – where her not knowing it is also a key part of the temptation. 'Save your honour', says Isabella, exiting with a conventional farewell, to which Angelo replies a second after she has gone: 'From thee: even from thy virtue!' He then has to ask himself: 'What's this? What's this?':

> The tempter or the tempted, who sins most, ha?
> Not she; nor dost she tempt; but it is I …
>
> *Measure for Measure*, 2.2.167–70

The very grammar of our minds seems to underwrite the assumption that the world is filled with independent and substantial objects with separate names: subject, verb, object. But grammar is odder than that in Shakespeare and needs more working out. Take the case of dramatic asides: as with soliloquy, Shakespeare goes beyond the basic theatrical use of giving separate information to the audience, even while incorporating it. When the disguised Edgar leads his father, the suicidal blind Gloucester, to the edge of a non-existent cliff, the aside may look primitively explicit and we may miss the language of a novel that can keep private thoughts privately interior: 'Why I do trifle thus with his despair | Is done to cure it' (*The Tragedy of King Lear*, 4.5.33–4). Yet by this means the stage is suddenly made a split screen, when the blind Gloucester, feet away, with heightened senses, cannot hear these words; the awkward speech has all the unbearable pain of a disguised son caught in terrible witness of a desperately risky process; and, above all, it is a thought that has to come out there, in the world, rightly taking its anomalous place amid the whole intervolved reality to which it so uncomfortably belongs and refers. The innerness is secondary, because it does indeed come second into the world that occasions it. There are energies in Shakespeare *before* there are characters, and when the characters are called into being, the forces that summon them still go on within and between them.

'Grief fills the room up of my absent child,' cries the bereft Lady Constance. 'Lies in his bed, walks up and down with me' (*King*

John, 3.4.93–4). 'Grief' there is functional shift writ large, writ close to metaphor and then again allegory in the sudden heterogeneous jump of terms from one place to quite another level. 'Grief' used to be a noun but is now indeed a person, to fill the vacuum in place of a lost son. What is inside Constance feels more like somebody missing outside her. Thus a character can say something and suddenly the whole surrounding world on stage changes – its boundaries, its structure, its very grammar and geometry of configuration. *There* are Hermione and Polixenes on one side of the stage, and *there* is jealous Leontes on the other, and again it is suddenly a split screen. It is a shock to recognize that what Leontes sees as coming from them is coming from him: the thought of Hermione as guilty is so verbally powerful that it virtually stands there alongside the innocent Hermione on stage, like another character coming out of one mind and trying to embody itself in its near likeness: 'You will not own it' (*The Winter's Tale*, 3.2.58). Or at the end of *Measure for Measure*, Mariana can call and call again for Isabella's intercession on behalf of Angelo, though the Duke says that 'against all sense you do importune her'. Mariana isn't just desperately asking her for help, 'Sweet Isabel, take my part'; she is seeing the vacant space that only Isabella can fill, though Isabella, as sister of the wronged Claudio, seems the last person who could fill it: 'Isabel, | Sweet Isabel, do yet but kneel by me', 'O Isabel, will you not lend a knee?' It isn't just the name, it is a language calling this Isabella into being, if Isabella herself will consent to be her (*Measure for Measure*, 5.1.427, 433–4, 439). Calling for Isabella here is like crying for mercy. And when Isabella does so suddenly consent, it is as if she were that Mercy which Angelo himself would not embody for her when she had urged it, 'And mercy then will breathe within your lips, | Like man made new' (2.2.80–1). Characters go in and out of each other here just as they do in the earlier more solid mistakings of one for another in *The Comedy of Errors*: 'the counterchange | Is severally in all' (*Cymbeline*, 5.5.397–8).

As it is in the reconfigurations of space, so it is in the shifts of time. This is a world of such powerful language that for Leontes, his son Mamilius 'dies to me again, when talk'd of' (*The Winter's Tale*, 5.1.119). So, similarly, when the disguised Edgar urges Gloucester to see from what a height he has fallen and yet been saved: 'Do but look up', Gloucester immediately must cry, 'Alack, I have no eyes' (*The Tragedy of King Lear*, 4.5.59–60) – and at that moment, in Shakespeare's cubist reality, Gloucester is blinded twice. It isn't just memory; effectively it happens again. And happens again when Gloucester cries piteously to mad Lear, 'Dost thou know me?' and hears in terrible response, 'I remember thine eyes well enough ... | No, do thy worst, blind Cupid. I'll not love. | Read thou this challenge. Mark but the penning of it.' And Gloucester is re-blinded, yet again, when he has to reply, 'Were all thy letters suns, I could not see' (4.5.131–6).

When there are these strange leaps in words and time and space within Shakespeare's universe, the rule is Ruskin's on our being faced with truths of apparently contradictory character: 'the essential thing for the reader is to receive their *truth*, however little he may be able to see their *consistency*'.[9] If they are truths and are openly received, they will eventually fit themselves together, making for a fuller world than we can consciously design. In other words, Ruskin's is like Abbott's account of the Shakespearean grammatical rule: take the mind before the syntax, the thought's truth before the thought's consistency. Do it first, make it first, accept it first. Shakespearean thinking is on behalf of the unpredictable and the unanticipatable, to which the mind must then adapt its structures and itself.

In conclusion, then, it is manifest that Shakespeare's is not a transparent, propositional, informational discourse. His is a language, in the deepest sense, that defies being taken over by the mind and placed in its comfortably pre-established patterns. Not only does the dense vocabulary at once resist and entice the mind, but the under-language of its very structures also enters the mind at pre-conceptual levels deep within the physical action of the brain itself. That is to say, putting together semantics and syntax, mind and brain, it *is* an irreducible language, a code of its own – not simply standing for something else but *being* that something else by making it emerge into meaningful existence again as from the very roots of its formation. I repeat what Berowne said of love, it 'gives to every power a *double* power, | Above their functions and their offices. | It adds a precious seeing to the eye' (*Love's Labour's Lost*, 4.3.307–9). Thus I have tried to show that it is not just his words that get into us; his language carries far into the brain all that is also resonantly held in the leaps, the gaps, the shapes and spaces between and round those words in the very act of formulation. That is what I think Hazlitt was gesturing towards when in 'On Shakspeare and Milton' he said that Shakespeare's language 'is hieroglyphical'. Only I say: you can't merely translate it, it gets into you. It seems partly to mirror and engage, partly to modify and mutate deep structures below consciousness, out of which we feel the process of consciousness re-forming itself in the emergent language. For the language as a whole is an 'it' – deeper than the characters or the situations that both surround it and emerge from it. Shakespeare can intuitively find or create those compelling situations – a father-king (Henry IV), a son (Hal), a quasi-father (Falstaff) and an alternative son-prince (Hotspur). And out of the spaces within those generative situations, he can re-create the conditions of consciousness coming into being – involving all levels of human action, in a mixture of premonition and chance that seems the fullest expression of life.

I began with talking about a lost language and the need to recover it. I come to a provisional end with the best account I know of why this sort of dynamic always has to be both lost and found, and cannot ever be held steadily in consciousness. It is the process by which humans astonish themselves.

In his book *Human Personality*, published posthumously in 1903, F. W. H. Myers describes the nature and function of genius.

It is, he says, '*a subliminal uprush*' (p. 56), 'the sudden creation of new cerebral connections or pathways' (p. 82). Myers argues that during our long evolutionary adaptation to new environments there has been a continual displacement of the 'threshold' or 'limen' of consciousness (p. 14). There are certain faculties that natural selection has 'lifted above' that threshold, for the working purposes of everyday existence (p. 77). Too often we think of these faculties as all there is and the level at which they operate as the primary one. But other powers, which were not called into consciousness as immediately useful, were stored 'subliminally', latently below consciousness, in a kind of dynamic memory (p. 14). It is these unseen powers that genius calls up from the subliminal level, to reunite them with consciousness. More than anyone else, we may conclude, it is Shakespeare who starts down at that deep pre-cognitive level, and brings everything up from there. Thus what is at stake in this present work is the necessary and vital role of Shakespeare in any modern re-education – enacting for us:

- what thinking dynamically is in action, as it comes into being from deep levels of formulation;
- how we too often forget this primary dramatic experience, in slower secondary forms of opinionated consciousness, which offer us false models both of self and of educated intellect;
- how, in the name of a deeper sense of originality, it does not matter that a thought has been thought before, if now it rushes into new linguistic being and surprises its own thinker, as though for the first time again.

And all this – at a time when literary criticism no longer appears to be a discipline at the forefront of human thinking, as it did perhaps in the 1930s, but instead too often seems like a secondary and explicatory activity – points towards a future for which this book is itself experiment and harbinger.

I have sought to remind readers of a primary way of thinking that can only be recalled through the dense immediacies of *literary* thinking, the dramatic action of thinking-out-in-language which is embodied above all in the poetry of Shakespeare's original texts. Those texts map out an accelerated story of the evolution of dynamic consciousness from the deep workings of language in the brain.

That is why at the University of Liverpool we are in the process of updating Myers' thoughts on subliminal uprush and, specifically, Abbott's lessons in functional shift by putting our students through MEG (Magnetoencephalograhy) and FMRI (Functional Magentic Resonance Imaging) brain-scanners, as well as using EEG (electroencephalogram) tests, with electrodes placed on different parts of the scalp. This is a collaboration with Professor Neil Roberts, the head of a unit entitled the 'Magnetic Resonance and Image Analysis Research Centre', to try to help re-create a natural philosophy that works between arts and sciences but is hard-wired and not merely metaphorical.

At this very early and rather primitive stage, we cannot initially give our student-subjects undiluted lines of Shakespeare because too much in the brain would light up in too many places: that is one of the definitions of what the Shakespeare-language does. So, the stimuli we are going to use are simply to do with the noun-to-verb or verb-to-noun shift-words themselves, with more ordinary language around them. It is not Shakespeare taken neat, it is just based on Shakespeare, with water. But we want to see what happens – in the language centres, in Broca's area, in Wernicke's region – when the brain comes upon sentences like 'The dancers *foot* it with grace', or 'We waited for *disclose* of news', or 'Strong wines *thick* my thoughts', or 'I could *out-tongue* your griefs' or 'Fall down and *knee* | The way into his mercy', and has no italics or emphases to go by in the shift-words 'foot' or 'disclose' or 'thick' or 'tongue' or 'knee'. Perhaps it will just seem inconclusively odd. But we will also want to investigate what if any brain-difference it might make for the subject to *see* the sentence and to *hear* the sentence. I do not seek to disguise the problems here or the danger of reductivism or the possible inconclusiveness of results and, as I write, we are still in the process of finalizing the initial procedures and the experiments. So, in this series of short books which are meant to have all the ruggedness of work in progress, here in particular you must imagine it as a possible thought-experiment.

The main cognitive research done so far on the confusion of verbs and nouns has been to do with mistakes made by those who are brain-damaged and thus on the possible neural correlates of grammatical errors and semantic violations. Hardly anybody appears to have investigated the neural processing of a 'positive error', such as functional shift in normal healthy organisms.[10] The grammatical shift should certainly fire the part of the brain concerned with syntactical anomalies: the question is whether it also recruits other shifts within the brain, whether it is truly a shift of function behind the eyes as well as in front of them – in the interrelation, for example, between syntax and semantics. This, then, is a chance to map something of what Shakespeare does to the mind at the level of brain, to catch the flash of lightning that makes for thinking. When a subject reads the test stimulus 'he godded me' in comparison with the control 'he treated me like a god', I expect the machinery to register a peak, a surge in neural excitement around that word 'godded'. For my guess, more broadly, is that Shakespeare's syntax, its shifts and movements, can lock into the existing pathways of the brain and actually move and change them – away from old habits and easy long-established sequences. It could be that Shakespeare's use of language gets so far into our brains that he shifts and creates new pathways – not unlike the establishment of new biological networks using novel combinations of existing elements (genes/proteins in biology: units of phonology, semantics, syntax, and morphology in language). Functional shift is a small but powerful example of that possibility.

The reason for simply isolating verb–noun or noun–verb shifts is this. Previous research suggests that there is a specific small area in the brain which processes verbs and a different small area that processes nouns. That is to say, there is here a neural substrate to experiment upon, and we will have simple control sentences alongside those containing functional shifts for purposes of comparison. Thus: what will happen when a word looks like a noun but functions like a verb? Will 'x', the noun-processing area, first light up and then be superseded by the lighting-up of 'y', the verb-processing area? Or, more likely, will there be a hesitation, measurable both in minute temporal terms and in terms of the recordable movement of the eye, no longer progressing easily on the line left to right? And with that predicted hesitation, as the repair mechanism sets in at the frontal lobes to re-create orientation, won't there be some corresponding discharge of affect, some feeling and emotion, registered in the right hemisphere? Scientists want hypotheses to test out. This forces someone such as myself to make predictions which normally I might be wary of. One of my specific guesses in this context is that it might make no difference whether the conversion is from noun to verb or from verb to noun: I think both movements are equally to do with (Hazlitt's key word) *action*. I am told that when the brain picks up the word 'knee', the part of the brain to do with moving the knee actually fires, albeit less powerfully than in the physical action itself. I, a life-long reader, had no idea that language could be so powerful. The brain could be a theatre, in rehearsal of life-actions, just as conversely actors on the stage could be like embodied thoughts working together. And in that theatre, the stage can be seen shifting its very shape in less than half a second.

Cognitive science is often to do with the discovery of the precise localization of functions. But suppose that instead we can show the following by neuro-imaging: that for all the localization of noun-processing in one place and the localization of verb-processing in another, when the brain is asked to work at more complex meanings, the localization gives way to the *movement between* the two static locations. Then the brain is working at a higher level of evolution, *un*determined by the structures it still works from. And then we might be rediscovering at a demonstrable neural level the experience not merely of specialist 'art' but of thinking itself going on not in static terms but in dynamic ones. We might be able to see within ourselves a changing neurological configuration of the brain, like the shape of the syntax just ahead of the realization of the semantics.

In that case, Shakespeare's art would be no more and no less than the supreme example of a mobile, creative and adaptive human capacity, in deep relation between brain and language. It makes new combinations, creates new networks, with changed circuitry and added levels, layers and overlaps. And all the time, it works like the cry of 'Action' on a film-set, by sudden peaks of activity and excitement dramatically breaking through into consciousness. It makes for what William James said of mind in his *Principles of Psychology*, 'a theatre of simultaneous possibilities'. Then to say that Shakespeare could make you more fully alive would not be an artsy rhetoric, vulnerable to seeming soft: it would be to do with Shakespeare's codes keying into the fundamental life-structures of the brain and raising them to new levels of interrelationship.

Notes

1 It is also an attempt to take some of the examples and findings of a previous work, *Sudden Shakespeare* (London: Athlone, 1996), into a further
experimental context.

2 In an unpublished paper of 1868, John Henry Newman gave the example of a person who believed that Aristotle had in his thinking the sort of
'fullness' that was not just capable of, but almost demanded, further
development even in the present. This person became someone who not
only had a near-complete knowledge of Aristotle's philosophy but also
absorbed it within, as a body of living thought. This learned Aristotelian,
Newman concluded, 'is one who can answer any whatever philosophical
questions in the way that Aristotle would have answered them'. But what
is more: 'if they are questions which could not occur in Aristotle's age, he
still answers them'. For Newman concludes, 'In one respect he knows
more than Aristotle, because in new emergencies after the time of
Aristotle, he can and *does* answer what Aristotle would have answered,
but for the want of opportunity did not' (quoted by Ian Kerr in the fore-
word to Newman's *Essay on the Development of Christian Doctrine* (Notre
Dame, IN: University of Notre Dame, 1989), p. xxiv). Of course, the
risk is always that this is not Aristotle, so much as this philosopher's distorted version or paraphrase of Aristotle, in the context of a quite different age. But Newman believes in the fundamental capability for
transmission and recognition, across time, through acts of writing and by
reading – where, for all the flaws and losses, there remains a compara-
tively high-percentage chance that something can be personally handed
on and personally taken over, which otherwise, without the existence of

literature, would be wholly lost with the death of the originating person concerned. Above all, Newman believes there are some texts and some thinkers so full as to contain within them the seeds of their own 'development', awaiting and summoning vehicles for the future unfolding of their implicit meaning.

3 But Dryden is closer to Shakespeare in his translation of Lucretius, for example on the most intimate of human relationships:

> They grip, they squeeze, their humid tongues they dart,
> As each would force their way to t'other's heart:
> In vain; they only cruise about the coast.
> For bodies cannot pierce, nor be in bodies lost:
> As sure they strive to be, when both engage,
> In that tumultuous momentary rage;
> So 'tangled in the nets of love they lie,
> Till man dissolves in that excess of joy ...
> A pause ensues ...
> Again they in each other would be lost,
> But still by adamantine bars are crossed.

This (quoted in William Kerrigan and Gordon Braden, *The Idea of the Renaissance* (Baltimore: Johns Hopkins University Press, 1989), p. 199) is what is called in Shakespeare's Sonnet 125 '*mutual render*, only me for thee' [my italics] – where what should be 'service' and 'exchange' is also involuntarily still 'rending' and 'tearing apart'. It is like a template for *Antony and Cleopatra*: for all the dissolution of fixed boundaries, for all the interpenetrating power of thought moving in and out of different bodies, there are, equally, impermeable physical barriers and frustratingly enticing biological limits inherent in the very structure and dynamic of this world-view. In Shakespeare in particular it is like the struggle for the infinite within the finite.

4 Herman Melville, 'Hawthorne and his Mosses' (1850) in John Gross, *After Shakespeare* (Oxford: Oxford University Press, 2002), p. 45.

5 See Philip Davis, 'The future in the instant': Hazlitt's *Essay* and Shakespeare' in U. Natarajan, T. Paulin and D. Wu (eds), *Metaphysical Hazlitt* (London: Routledge 2005), pp. 43–55.

6 So, in Hazlitt's *Lectures on the English Poets* Shakespeare, it is argued, does

not work by 'a set speech or two, a preconcerted theory of a character' ('On Poetry in General'); rather, 'all the persons concerned must have been present in the poet's imagination, as at a kind of rehearsal' ('On Shakspeare and Milton').

7 *The Complete Works of William Hazlitt*, ed. P. P. Howe, 21 vols (London and Toronto: J. M. Dent, 1930–4), vol. xviii, 305–6.

8 'In Shakespeare's time and country, to be religious already began to mean to be Puritanical; and in the divorce between the fullness of life, on the one hand, and the depth and unity of faith, on the other, there could be no doubt as to which side a man of imaginative instincts would attach himself ... A world of passion and beauty without a meaning must seem to him more interesting and worthy than a world of empty principle and dogman, meagre, fanatical and false', *Selected Critical Writings of George Santayana*, ed. Norman Henfrey, 2 vols (Cambridge: Cambridge University Press, 1968), 1, p. 69. It is true that 'Dost thou think because thou art virtuous there shall be no more cakes and ale?' (*Twelfth Night*, 2.3.110–11) is one of Shakespeare's clarion calls, but the nature of the experiment is precisely not to know in advance whether there is indeed 'meaning' amidst so much that seems to call for it.

9 *The Renaissance Philosophy of Man*, ed. E. Cassirer, P. O. Kristeller and J. H. Randall (Chicago, IL: University of Chicago Press, 1948), pp. 224–5.

10 'There is great significance in this for the actor. All sorts of acting choices open up when a decision not to treat as metaphor any reference to an organ of the body is accompanied by the experience of thought and word in the organ itself', Kristin Linklater, *Freeing Shakespeare's Voice* (New York: Theatre Communications Group, 1992), p. 58.

11 See Michael Witmore, *Culture of Accidents* (Stanford, CA: Stanford University Press, 2001), especially Introduction and Chapter 1.

Chapter 2

1 See *Coleridge on Shakespeare*, ed. T. Hawkes (Harmondsworth, Middlesex: Penguin, 1969), p. 229 (from a report by P. Collier of a lecture on *The Tempest* by Coleridge, 1811–12).

2 *Renaissance Philosophy* vol. 1: The Italian philosophers, ed. and trans. by A. B. Fallico and H. Shapiro (New York: The Modern Library, 1967), pp. 367–8. See also my *Sudden Shakespeare* (London: Athlone, 1996), Chapter 1.

3 See Bruce R. Smith, *The Acoustic World of Early Modern England* (Chicago: University of Chicago, 1999), p. 117 (1630s commonplace book: Folger MS V.a.345).

4 See David Constantine, 'Finding the words' in *In Other Words: the journal for literary translators*, no. 13/14, autumn/winter 1999/2000, pp. 10–22. It is as though the poem – or what it seeks to represent – is in some sense already there: 'Trying to write a poem, the space you are staring into will in the end, if you are lucky, begin to fill with words. The space becomes a shape. But you need to be quite peculiarly lucky. The words taking shape may be the wrong words. They may be *in the way of*, not on the way towards the poem ... Then you would prefer the space to the shape, blankness to fullness' (p. 11).

5 George T. Wright, 'Hendiadys and *Hamlet*', reprinted from PMLA (1981), 168–93, in V. Salmon and E. Burness (eds), *A Reader in the Language of Shakespearean Drama* (Amsterdam and Philadelphia: John Benjamins, 1987), p. 420. Simon Palfrey's interest in split-second cues, in how the actor has to make his character's existence a thing secured between and amid passing speech-acts, is important here, as will be shown in his forthcoming book on cues, co-authored with Tiffany Stern, to be published by Oxford University Press.

6 G. Bullough (ed.), *Narrative and Dramatic Sources of Shakespeare, volume 2: The Comedies, 1597–1603* (London: Routledge and Kegan Paul, 1963), pp. 357–63.

7 George T. Wright, *Shakespeare's Metrical Art* (Berkeley: University of California Press, 1988), p. 257. He also quotes as an epigraph some words on Darwin's revolution, 'Darwin revolutionized our study of nature by taking the actual variation among actual things as central to

the reality, not as an annoying and irrelevant disturbance to be wished away' (p. xv). And later he puts it thus, 'In effect, two forces contend in Shakespeare's verse: the force of life and the force of pattern. From one point of view, pattern *is* life … But pattern may also be neat and trivial … and from it the vigorous and insistent human force rebels and flinches, asserts its powerful individuality in exceptional action and verse. Departure is character' (p. 282). Yet, of course, the departure is also a part of a newer, larger pattern too in the expanded life of the plays.

8　Thus Thomas More on the 'removal' of strangers from our shores (here quoted with modernized spelling but unmodernized quasi-physiological punctuation):

> grant them removed and grant that this your noise
> hath chid down all the majesty of England
> imagine that you see the wretched strangers
> their babies at their backs, with their poor luggage
> plodding to th' ports and coasts for transportation
> and that you sit as kings in your desires
> authority quite silenced by your brawl
> and you in ruff of your opinions clothed
> what had you got ∴ I'll tell you, you had taught
> how insolence and strong hand should prevail
> how order should be quelled, and by this pattern
> not one of you should live an aged man
> for other ruffians as their fancies wrought
> with selfsame hand self reasons and self right
> would shark on you and men like ravenous fishes
> would feed on one another

There are three commas throughout, signalling minor pauses, and one major pause at the argument's turning point signalled by the idiosyncratic notation of three pricks (Bruce R. Smith, *The Acoustic World of Early Modern England*, pp. 110–11; Stanley Wells and Gary Taylor (eds), *William Shakespeare: A Textual Companion* (Oxford: Clarendon Press, 1987), pp. 465–6).

9 'The neuro-physiological pathways connecting words with the sensory apparatus of the body and with nature have not disappeared, but they have been short-circuited as the technology of communication has "progressed"', Kristin Linklater, *Freeing Shakespeare's Voice* (New York: Theatre Communications Group, 1992), p. 13.

10 Paul Broks, *Into The Silent Land* (London: Atlantic Books, 2003), pp. 79–80.

11 John Dewey, *Philosophy and Civilization* (New York: Minton, Blach, 1931), p. 120.

12 Henri Bergson, *Creative Evolution*, translated by Arthur Mitchell (London: Macmillan, 1914), p. 49.

13 For purposes of recognition, here is an example of such thinking in a different and slower contemporaneous context. In the first stanza of 'The Flower' Herbert tells of how he has got over his long, many-winter-like depression, which has disappeared at last so suddenly. But the second stanza starts from the opposite pole of unbelief: if now he cannot believe he ever had it, before he could not believe he would ever get over it:

> Grief melts away
> Like snow in May,
> As if there were no such cold thing.
>
> Who would have thought my shrivel'd heart
> Could have recover'd greennesse? It was gone
> Quite under ground ...

The apparently static conventional space between the two stanzas we retrospectively see to have been active and dramatic, to have yielded an inner voice productive of that new, unpredictable turn of memory. 'Who would have thought' it? The thought at the beginning of the second stanza, like the deliverance, seems to come from nowhere; yet *when* it has come, you can also see where it has come *from* – and that is indeed what makes you see that it was indeed *thought*. This is Shakespearean live-thinking – living forwards in a way that recreates the past behind itself and makes for further life ahead.

Chapter 3

1 E. A. Abbott *Flatland: A Romance of Many Dimensions* (London: Penguin, 1998), p. 108.

2 Peter Brook, *Evoking Shakespeare* (London: Nick Hern Books, 1998), p. 12 (adapted).

3 Donald Davie, *Articulate Energy* (London: Routledge and Kegan Paul, 1976), p. 35

4 See George T. Wright, 'Hendiadys and *Hamlet*', *PMLA* 96 (1981), 168–91, reprinted in V. Salmon and E. Burgess (eds), *A Reader in the Language of Shakespearean Drama* (Amsterdam and Philadelphia: John Benjamins, 1987), especially p. 408.

5 See on early modern hysteria in particular Janet Adelman, *Suffocating Mothers* (London: Routledge, 1992), Gail Kern Paster, *The Body Embarrassed* (Ithaca: Cornell, 1993).

6 Gillian Beer, *Open Fields* (Oxford: Oxford University Press, 1996), p. 210: the quotation from Tyndall follows on p. 211.

7 See Sylvia Adamson's fine chapter 'Literary Language' in *The Cambridge History of the English Language*, vol. 3: 1476–1776, ed. Roger Lass, especially pp. 550, 584–93 on turns and periods.

8 See above, Chapter 1 of this present volume, pp. 31–4.

9 *Modern Painters*, vol. 5, 1860, part 9, Chapter 5, footnote to paragraph 22.

10 But see Vivien C. Tartter *et al.*, 'Novel Metaphors' in *Brain and Language* 80 (2004), 488–509. Preliminary results from Liverpool experiments are recorded in *The Reader*, no. 23 (Autumn 2006) pp. 39–43.

Index

Milton Keynes UK
Ingram Content Group UK Ltd.
UKHW012337290124
436950UK00011B/247